MISSION FIRST PEOPLE ALWAYS

What It Means to Be a Two-part Leader

Capt. Daniel Johnston

Mission First, People Always
Copyright © 2021 Daniel Johnston

All rights reserved.

ISBN: 979-8-4728-5316-3

First Edition

www.emergingink.com

Without limiting the rights under copyright reserved above, no part of this publication may be reproduced, stored in or introduced into a retrieval system, or transmitted in any form or by any means (electronic, mechanical, photocopying, recording, or otherwise), without the prior written permission of the author except in case of brief quotations embodied in critical articles and reviews.

Because of the dynamic nature of the Internet, any web addresses or links contained in this book may have changed since publication and may no longer be valid.

Names and identifying details have been changed to protect individuals' privacy.

To Amanda and Henry,
who have shown me the true meaning of strength.

TABLE OF CONTENTS

INTRODUCTION 1
    THE TWO-PART LEADER 4

1. COMMUNICATION 9
    PROVIDE FEEDBACK 10
        With Great Power Comes Great Responsibility 11
        Lincoln's Unsent Letter 13
    SET CLEAR EXPECTATIONS 15
        NASA's Blunder 15
        Raising the Bar 17
    SHARE ORGANIZATIONAL GOALS 18
        Unorganized Labor 18
        "I Have a Dream." 19
    SHARE ORGANIZATIONAL SUCCESS 20
        "We Shall Go on to the End." 21
    SHARE ORGANIZATIONAL NEEDS 23
        Saving Face 24
        The Jewish Queen of Persia 25
    COMMUNICATION REFLECTION QUESTIONS 27

2. DELEGATION 28
    FOCUS ON LEADING 29
        Understanding Your Role 30
        Lawn-Chair Leadership 31
    PRIORITIZE YOUR WORK 32
        Forming a Functional Team 32
        They Shall Bear the Burden with Thee 33
    RECOGNIZE THE STRENGTHS OF YOUR PEOPLE 35
        The Great War Against Buggers 35
    MAKE CLEAR ASSIGNMENTS 37
        "There's Always Money in the Banana Stand." 37
        They Hadn't Advertised – at All 38
    EMPOWER YOUR PEOPLE 40
        Edison vs. Tesla 40
        The Universal Ruler 42
    DON'T OVERLOAD YOUR PEOPLE 43
        Spreading the Wealth 43
        Burnout 44
    DELEGATION REFLECTION QUESTIONS 46

3. FOLLOW-UP 48

ASSIGN MEANINGFUL WORK 49
   The 440 Test 49
   The Joys of Busywork 51
ATTENTION TO DETAIL 52
   That Guy's a Machine 52
   Winging It 54
BE INVESTED 55
   Ignorance Isn't Always Bliss 55
   The Weight of Command 56
ASK EFFECTUAL QUESTIONS 57
   Putting Issues Under the Microscope 58
   Like a Fine-Tooth Comb 59
LISTEN TO AND ACT ON ANSWERS 60
   O-Ring Disaster 61
   For the Greater Good 62

4. TIME MANAGEMENT 65

BE INTENTIONAL WITH HOW YOU SPEND YOUR TIME 66
   No Detail Too Small 66
   Walk the Line 67
VALUE TIME AS A RESOURCE, YOURS AS WELL AS OTHERS 68
   "In a Gentle Way, You Can Shake the World" 69
PRIORITIZE WHAT DESERVES YOUR ATTENTION 70
   Good, Better, Best 70
   The Eisenhower Matrix 71
MAKE TIME TO TALK TO YOUR PEOPLE 73
   "Impossible Things Are Happening Every Day." 73
   Airmen Breakfast 74
TAKE TIME TO PLAN, THINK, AND DEVELOP 74
   Time Out 75
   The OODA Loop 75
   Use the Force! 77

5. HOW TO ENFORCE STANDARDS 81

RECOGNIZE THE IMPORTANCE OF STANDARDS 83
   "This Lamb Is So Undercooked…" 83
   "Some Day My Prince Will Come…" 84
INCREASE STANDARDS TO INCREASE PERFORMANCE 85
   Continuous Improvement Process 86
   Miracle on Ice 87
CREATE A CULTURE THROUGH ENFORCING STANDARDS 88
   Leave It to the Chief 89
   Semper Fi 89
   My Pleasure! 90
USE STANDARDS TO CREATE A SAFE ENVIRONMENT 91

  Chernobyl, 1986 .... *92*
  Betrayal of Trust *93*
 DO NOT ALLOW EXCEPTIONS FROM STANDARDS 94
  The Honor Code *94*
  Harvard's Diversity Problem *95*
 ALLOW YOURSELF FLEXIBILITY IN ENFORCEMENT 96
  Letter of the Law *97*
  Allowing Creativity in Discipline *97*
 HOW TO ENFORCE STANDARDS REFLECTION QUESTIONS 100

6. VISION 105

 CREATE A CLEAR PATH TO YOUR VISION 106
  Fork in the Road *106*
  Marvel vs. DC *107*
  Safe and Reliable *109*
 A VISION IS MORE THAN A PLAN 110
  "First to the Key, First to the Egg!" *110*
  Campaigns That Became Movements *111*
 YOUR VISION SHOULD SEIZE FUTURE OPPORTUNITIES 112
  Father of the Air Force *113*
  Blockbuster's Downfall *114*
 YOUR VISION SHOULD NAVIGATE FUTURE PITFALLS 116
  First Line of Defense *116*
  "And Then We'll Teach Them How to Say Goodbye." *117*
 VISION REFLECTION QUESTIONS 119

7. TRICKLE-DOWN ATTITUDE 120

 UNDERSTAND HOW YOUR ATTITUDE 121
  When the Captain's Not Happy, Nobody's Happy *122*
  The Patriot Way *123*
 RECOGNIZE THE CONTRIBUTIONS OF YOUR PEOPLE 125
  The Creation of a Traitor *125*
  Victory Friday *127*
  Get Out from Behind Your Desk *128*
 INSPIRE YOUR ORGANIZATION TO PUSH THROUGH CHALLENGES 129
  Visions of Nature *129*
  Alexander the Great, Lord of Asia *130*
 MAINTAIN CONTROL THROUGH CHAOS 132
  The Skipper Always Knows What to Do *132*
  A Citadel of Freedom *134*
 TRICKLE-DOWN ATTITUDE REFLECTION QUESTIONS 136

8. LIVE YOUR PRINCIPLES 137

 YOU ARE THE FACE OF YOUR ORGANIZATION 138
  Door-to-Door Sales *139*

Heir Apparent *140*
Your Every Move Is Observed 141
    Presidential Politics *141*
    A Battle Worth Fighting *142*
Your Personal Character Matters 144
    Scandal in the Deep South *144*
    The Prince of Peace *145*
Dependability Is the Basis of Trust 146
    The Boy Who Lived *147*
    Thinking Man's General *149*
Decide What Principles Will Influence... 150
    A One-Way Conversation *151*
Live Your Principles Reflection Questions 153

9. GET TO KNOW YOUR PEOPLE 154

Make the Effort to Build Relationships 155
    Walking a Mile in Their Shoes *156*
    Swing-Shift Stopovers *157*
    Charging the Hill *159*
Find Out What Matters to Your People 160
    The Difference a Conversation Can Make *161*
    Becoming a Man of the People *162*
Build Your People Through Mentoring 163
    Diamond in the Rough *163*
Maintain Healthy Boundaries 166
    "I Want People to Be Afraid of..." *166*
    Drawing a Line *167*
Get to Know Your People Reflection Questions 170

10. SERVE YOUR PEOPLE 171

Do Not Use Your Position to Obtain... 172
    "I Just Knew It Wasn't the Right Thing to Do." *172*
    "Be Prepared!" *174*
Remember the Purpose of Your Authority 176
    The Watergate Scandal *176*
Give People the Tools They Need to Succeed 178
    Turning Students into Leaders *179*
    Ford's Most Valuable Asset *180*
Servant Leadership Will Build Motivation 182
    The Inverted Pyramid *182*
    The 10-Hour Rule *184*
Measure Your Success 185
    "I Am Spartacus!" *185*
    The Ultimate Sacrifice *187*
Serve Your People Reflection Questions 189

11. THE FINAL CHALLENGE **190**
 Lean on What You Know, Build What You Don't 190
 What Kind of Leader Will You Be? 192
APPENDIX **197**
 Air Force Maintenance Organizational Structure 197
 Air Force Rank Hierarchy 198
NOTES **199**

INTRODUCTION

For most of my youth, I served in leadership roles within the organizations that I participated in, such as Boy Scouts, church, lacrosse, football, and academic clubs like National Honors Society. These opportunities convinced me I was a good leader. How could I not be with all of this experience?

Confident in my leadership ability, I entered the Reserve Officer Training Corp (ROTC) program at my university. Like many other freshmen cadets who had enrolled, I knew nothing about the Air Force. During my years in ROTC, I gained insight into who and what a leader should be and obtained valuable experience training younger students, guiding them down paths I'd already taken. I felt prepared, knowledgeable, and ready to move on to the next step in my life: becoming an officer.

As a recent college graduate, I headed to my first assignment as a maintenance officer at Luke Air Force Base in Phoenix, Arizona. When I arrived, I was given the position of flight commander over the Fabrication Flight in the 56th Maintenance Group. This team was responsible for sheet metal repair, low observable coatings maintenance, and inspections for over 155 aircraft. Surely my training had prepared me to take on whatever challenges the Air Force had in store.

Soon after I took command, however, I realized leadership roles outside of the structured programs I was used to might not be so effortless. In fact, it was far more daunting to command over 140 airmen who made up the Fabrication Flight – 80% of whom were older than me and more experienced in Air Force maintenance operations. In past circumstances, I became a leader because I'd worked my way up and earned that position; I knew I was qualified to be the leader as did everyone under me. But my first year in command was challenging due to a lack of confidence in my own ability to lead. How could I tell my people what to do

Introduction

while having less experience and time under my belt? My insecurity drove me to defer most decision making to my senior enlisted flight chiefs.

A few months into my time as flight commander, I had an epiphany that transformed my entire outlook: while every leader should do what they can to obtain a greater understanding of their organization's operations, technical knowledge is not all that's needed to be effective or successful. I noticed this more frequently as I transitioned to different organizations. The foundation of proper leadership involves a completely different skillset that needs to be learned and developed.

This concept – that leadership requires its own skillset, one that each individual must focus on evolving – is the heart of this book. Many people find themselves in leadership roles without knowing what it takes to direct an organization or the people within it. Honestly, they might feel like I did: overwhelmed and unqualified for the assignment before them.

Feelings of inadequacy span across various industries and stem, not from a lack of vocational training, but from a lack of how to effectively lead their people. Perhaps you excelled in your field and were promoted because of your outstanding work. You might find yourself unprepared for a new position of management. You had always innately done well, but lack the skills or training to supervise, which creates anxiety.

Maybe you are a college graduate who recently entered the workforce. You probably led group projects at school, but now are responsible for guiding people with more than a grade on the line. You want to make the transition from a candidate with potential to a leader with confidence, though you don't have a clear roadmap how to get there.

It could even be you want to start a non-profit organization. You are dedicated to the community and desire a way to make a real impact on the issues. While you have never led any kind of institution before, you are energized and ready to learn.

This lack of basic leadership training and education is an issue that companies across America are already aware of and worry about. With 10,000 Baby Boomers retiring each day, organizations recognize the people they have relied on for years now need to be replaced. These substitutes must be prepared to meet the new challenges that face people today. New and young leaders occupy positions at every level, and 58% of businesses say that closing the leadership skill gap is their top priority. The issue is that only 5% of organizations have fully implemented development programs at all levels.[1]

Everyone recognizes this needs to change and leadership training must occur, but organizations often fail to make it happen or provide resources. Since a lack of guidance doesn't usually bring all operations to a screeching halt, it tends to fall by the wayside. It then becomes the sole responsibility of newly-promoted individuals to educate themselves on how to adequately manage. Those who accept this challenge will see that as they better understand how to lead people, their organization's performance and productivity will improve significantly.

One of the difficulties that organizations face in providing supervisors with training is deciding *how* to do so. Leadership is a topic that has been explored by scholars for over a century. What are the traits and skills that make a person a strong leader? This is a difficult question to answer regardless of industry, culture, or position. I found my own response while trying to solve a less abstract issue.

In 2014, aircraft inspections at Luke AFB found one of the F-16s had a crack in its longeron. This posed a serious issue because that component is the backbone of the aircraft. With the extreme amount of g-force put on an F-16 every time it flies, any structural issues with the longeron could potentially result in the aircraft splitting midflight. Not long before it was discovered that these cracks were a fleet-wide problem, we rendered a substantial portion of the aircraft non-airworthy until repairs could be made. My aircraft maintenance unit (AMU) was responsible for

Introduction

providing safe aircrafts for the F-16 pilots to train with – and we struggled to meet mission requirements with so many of our vehicles out of commission. It felt as though we were kicking as hard as we could, but were barely able to keep our heads above water. I faced difficult choices as I contemplated various solutions on how to improve our production.

With this on my mind, I spoke to my squadron commander, Major Wilson, about my options. I presented her with the possibilities I had considered, such as implementing a weekend duty crew, increasing the length of shifts, and even telling the group commander that we needed to lower the production of training missions. Maj. Wilson provided interesting and practical advice, but one statement she made impacted my view on leadership more than anything any mentor had ever said to me: *mission first, people always.*

This mantra is one deeply rooted in the U.S. military, dating back decades in both the Army and the Air Force.[2] Such a simple adage serves as a guiding principle for military officers as they approach difficult decisions throughout their careers. Beyond reminding me of my duties as an officer, these four words illustrated a formula for what it took to be a successful leader. It planted the seed for the idea that would grow into the concept of the two-part leader.

The Two-Part Leader

A two-part leader is an individual who utilizes both disciplines of management and motivation in guiding their people. This kind of leader understands the importance of having optimized processes as well as knowing how to inspire others to reach their full potential. While my experience stems from the military, each of us can become successful two-part leaders in any organization based on the Air Force's expectation of "mission first, people always."

MISSION FIRST, PEOPLE ALWAYS

Let's break it down first. The former part of the phrase – "mission first" – speaks to the necessity of a leader being able to effectively regulate their organization with resources. Management is what some companies focus on when they talk about leadership because proper oversight often leads to accomplishing goals and completing tasks on time. While being a good manager is an essential part of being a proper leader, that alone does not touch on all essential aspects of leadership.

For example, some managers pride themselves for doing their work promptly and thoroughly; they see their most pressing responsibilities as cutting waste and increasing productivity. To this type of leader, developing the skillset of a motivator may seem unproductive.

The second part of the phrase – "people always" – speaks to the necessity for a leader to care for and to inspire their people. Effective motivators are often the great leaders you read about in history books or the ones you watch in movies with underdog sports teams. Those who possess this skill connect with their people easily and get the most out of them because they provide opportunities for personal development. This results in a more satisfied organization. When a leader is attuned to the needs of their team and fights for essential resources, discontent is rare. However, a person who solely focuses on being a great motivator will have many friends within their organization but will consistently underperform.

A motivator is usually a very social person who accomplishes a lot through cultivating meaningful relationships with those they work alongside. They see their purpose geared toward creating a positive environment and empowering each person at an individual level. To this sort of leader, developing management attributes constrains them and doesn't allow them to reach their team in the way that they want to.

Each of us leans more toward one of these roles based on our natural tendencies. We often believe our inherent skills and strengths are more valuable to an organization than stepping outside of our comfort zones and establishing new methods. The truth is, however, that an organization cannot reach its full

Introduction

potential without a leader who is both a manager and a motivator. Being a two-part leader takes conscious effort because very few people innately have all the skills it requires to be successful in leadership positions.

This book identifies the attributes and techniques I've witnessed in two-part leaders. To better teach you the traits that comprise both management and motivation, I'll draw from my own experience as a young officer in the Air Force, that of others, and how I was able to learn lessons from both. You'll also find examples from history, sports, business, pop culture, film, and literature.

In highlighting these examples, I am not trying to convince you that any of these people, especially myself, are perfect leaders. Instead, I aim to demonstrate how these leadership principles are applicable across all disciplines of life; they are used in various situations, such as becoming a new manager at a restaurant, entering the corporate world, joining a new company, or transitioning to lieutenant-rank in the Air Force.

Each chapter contains questions at the end to help you better understand how to utilize each of these traits and guidelines in your own career.

MISSION FIRST

Effective management of your organization

1
COMMUNICATION

As a newly-promoted captain, I was soon deployed to Afghanistan. To prepare for every imaginable overseas situation I could potentially encounter, I attended multiple classes and trainings before leaving. One of these pre-deployment courses centered around the relationship of the U.S. and its representatives with the host nation. We studied the proper customs and courtesies to use while interacting with foreign officials, and we learned about the role of our military presence in the diplomatic relationships we had with those countries.

Our program included a mix of ranks, ranging from technical sergeant all the way to colonel. Everyone present was expected to share their unfiltered opinions in order to learn from each other as well as the instructor. One of our best discussions occurred during a lesson about how the Department of Defense (DoD) assists host countries with terrorism in their respective borders.

One of the officers had an issue with statements the DoD put out regarding their approach toward terrorism. He felt they were too tepid, that they failed to demonstrate the seriousness the U.S. should show toward eradicating terrorism in these regions. This individual believed more powerful vocabulary would promote a long-lasting impact.

"The strongest wording America has ever used is that they will 'degrade' or 'deter' terrorism in any country. Why not come out and say that we're going to *destroy* them? I don't see the point of simply degrading or deterring terrorism," he said, frustrated with the calculating nature of these past assertions.

Communication

Another officer who had recently returned from an assignment in an overseas embassy recognized the value of the American response. He explained that statements about wiping terrorism off the face of the Earth, while tempting, would prove counterproductive for the U.S. and the host country. It set the DoD up for failure by outlining unrealistic goals. Unfortunately, terrorism will always survive where there are evil people who want power; thus, these comments would give the citizens of the foreign country false hope of a utopia they cannot achieve.

Our instructor took a backseat for several minutes, acting as a moderator to the opinions and experience of the service members as students went back and forth. His face showed a mixed expression of intrigue and amusement as the debate ensued. As the topic reached its conclusion, he added only one thing to the conversion before moving on: "Words matter."

Communication lies at the core of two-part leadership, whether it's interpersonal, within a company, or statements to an entire nation. The words leaders choose have a profound effect on the actions of those on the receiving. Those who wish to become two-part leaders take the responsibility to be able to communicate effectively seriously. They understand it is the first step for any organization to successfully work together.

Provide Feedback

Feedback is a useful tool for leaders to communicate on an individual basis. It should occur during a set time where the focus is on one person and their needs to succeed in their position or with the company. Giving constructive criticism helps leaders make sure they're on the same page as their people. When they provide it, supervisors can clarify any misunderstandings and honestly evaluate their team's performance.

MISSION FIRST, PEOPLE ALWAYS

This type of conversation is frequently pushed aside for those who are doing well because it is assumed they don't need it. Leaders must let their people, who are exceeding expectations, know how much they're appreciated. Without this, employees start feeling unseen and resentful. During meetings or reviews, a leader can gain insight into the goals their team has both within the organization and as individuals. If an individual feels as though their lead has shown interest in them, they are more likely to stay in their position.

The most difficult type of feedback is that given to those who are not living up to performance standards. This can be frightening if you aren't used to confronting others in your everyday life, but it has to be done for the good of the team. If a leader wants to keep the unsatisfactory member in their organization, they can't just criticize them; instead, they must find solutions for the individual to correct their behavior and move forward with their work.

Officers in the Air Force are required to complete a feedback session with the officers and senior enlisted airmen (SNCOs) they supervise. As a lieutenant, I depended on my commander's feedback to guide me in what was expected of my presence and performance on the job. I was overwhelmed with everything I had to learn and my responsibilities since I was so new to the Air Force. I knew I could not possibly do it all at once, which is why these conversations told me what to prioritize.

Not only did we review the work I'd been doing, but we also discussed ways to improve as an officer. My commander asked me about my personal and career goals; he cared about how I adjusted from college life to the workforce and if I had the support I needed. I always left such sessions uplifted and ready to rededicate myself to my job. That's the goal of feedback between a leader and their people: to connect and push together toward greater achievement.

With Great Power Comes Great Responsibility

In Sam Raimi's 2002 movie *Spider-Man*, Peter Parker is a mild-mannered, nerdy high school student before being bit by a radioactive spider. Soon after, Peter exhibits unnatural powers like super strength, inhuman agility, the ability to scale walls, and an additional sense to alert him of nearby danger. His new skills initially allow him to fight back against Flash Thompson, the bully tormenting him. This feat helps impress his classmates, including Mary Jane, the girl he has had a crush on for years.

But Peter quickly takes the ambitions for his powers beyond standing up to school bullies as he decides to use his new powers for personal gain. He signs up for a wrestling competition where he is required to last three minutes in the ring with a wrestler named Bone Saw. If he lasts the listed amount of time, he wins $3,000, enough money to buy a car and potentially take Mary Jane on a date.

Peter continues his misbehavior and asks Uncle Ben, his legal guardian, to take him to the library, which is conveniently located near the wrestling. Unbeknownst to the high schooler, Uncle Ben has picked up on Peter's out-of-character tendencies and subsequently delivers to Peter one of the most influential pieces of feedback of his life:

Uncle Ben: We haven't talked at all for so long. Your Aunt May and I don't even know who you are anymore. You shirk your chores, you have all those weird experiments in your room, you start fights at school…

Peter: I didn't start that fight. I told you that.

Uncle Ben: Well, you sure as hell finished it… Peter, these are the years a man changes into the man he is going to become the rest of his life. Just be careful who you change into… This guy, Flash Thompson, he probably deserved what happened, but just because you can beat him up doesn't give you the right to. Remember: with great power comes great responsibility.[3]

MISSION FIRST, PEOPLE ALWAYS

Peter reflects on his uncle's words over and over again; that feedback from a man he perceives as a father figure resonates deeply within him. Ultimately, he decides to use his powers to help others, just like his uncle would want. He becomes Spiderman, a superhero dedicated to fighting crime and protecting the weak.

Uncle Ben serves as an example to how leaders need to give feedback to those they are responsible for. A parent or leader needs to be direct about where they stand with their people; if someone isn't living up to expectations, they need to know. At the same time, leaders should find ways to improve their performance. Uncle Ben modeled being firm with Peter while also encouraging him to live up to his potential. It's unproductive for both the leader and the person receiving feedback if there's a lack of transparency and no paths to progress are provided.

For constructive criticism to fulfill its intended purpose, leaders need to enter it with the sole intention of helping their people reach their highest capability. Those who understand this will be able to use their team to their benefit. People in leadership roles who utilize feedback to punish subordinates for their mistakes will miss out on opportunities to improve their organization and company morale. Feedback should be completely centered around your people and how you, as a leader, can guide individuals.

Lincoln's Unsent Letter

The Battle of Gettysburg was one of the central conflicts in the U.S. Civil War and the most significant (and bloodiest) battle in the country's history. Over 50,000 Americans died the day[4] General Meade led Union troops to this important triumph, halting General Lee's march into the North. This conflict is best known as the turning point of the Civil War, giving the Union much-needed momentum to obtain an eventual victory.

What is less well-known is that the Battle of Gettysburg was also a lost opportunity for the North to end the war outright. During his retreat, General Lee and the Confederate Army found themselves unable to cross the Potomac River due to a storm that

Communication

had caused the waterway to swell. The Confederates were trapped. President Lincoln commanded General Meade to overtake their opponents and end the war. For one reason or another, General Meade stalled, eventually allowing General Lee and his men to cross the river and prolong the war.[5]

When General Meade failed to seize this chance, President Lincoln was furious. To have a brilliant strategist like General Lee nearby and at a complete disadvantage was not an opportunity the Union forces were likely to have again. President Lincoln understood that the cost of this failure would be the loss of more soldiers' lives. He immediately set out to remind General Meade of the impact of his blunder to his country in the following letter.

> My Dear General,
>
> I do not believe you appreciate the magnitude of the misfortune involved in Lee's escape. He was within our easy grasp, and to have closed upon him would, in connection with our other late successes, have ended the war. As it is, the war will be prolonged indefinitely. If you could not safely attack Lee last Monday, how can you possibly do so south of the river, when you can take with you very few—no more than two-thirds—of the force you then had in hand? It would be unreasonable to expect, and I do not expect that you can now affect much. Your golden opportunity is gone, and I am distressed immeasurably because of it.[6]

After writing this letter, President Lincoln realized that if he sent it, he would lose General Meade to anger and resentment. It was his responsibility as a leader to maintain his composure and do what was best for the country. President Lincoln acknowledged that those with influence must use feedback wisely: to help their people improve, not satisfy their own frustrations. That is why this document never made it to General Meade and was found buried among President Lincoln's papers in his desk drawer after his death.

Feedback is an opportunity for leaders to make sure they're aligned in understanding and purpose with those they oversee. When criticism is done sincerely and effectively – by highlighting the strengths of people as well as the improvements that can be made – it makes all the difference to those within an organization, large or small. It imparts unto them a renewed vision of their performance and potential avenues to better themselves.

Constructive criticism provided effectively opens a channel of honest communication between a leader and their people. If not done at all or given without true consideration, it can blunder morale and harm the overall flow of communication.

Set Clear Expectations

A basic part of communicating for a leader is setting expectations for their organization. This means informed people know how their performance will be evaluated and what is required from them. When people have a clear idea of what they're supposed to be doing, there is a higher probability of them meeting said goals and standards.

NASA's Blunder

In the early 1990s, NASA began the Mars exploration mission, whose second phase would include launching the Mars Climate Orbiter (MCO). The objective of this multi-mission project was to explore the Martian climate in greater detail than before in the hopes of finding water. The purpose of the MCO was to orbit Mars, study its climate from above, and serve as a communication relay for the Mars Polar Lander, which was supposed to be sent off three weeks later.

When the MCO began its final approach, the plan was for the satellite to perform an orbital insertion followed by a two week "aero-braking" process. This would allow the MCO to reduce the velocity it had maintained on its travels through space and move into a circular Martian orbit. Due to the altered trajectory recognized earlier in the journey, however, the MCO was much closer to the planet than the NASA team intended. During the initial orbital insertion burn, NASA lost contact with the satellite.[7]

NASA was embarrassed to have lost the $193 million satellite on a high-profile mission and not have an answer for why it happened. After an internal investigation, NASA released the root cause for the mission failure: units of measurement. They primarily operated with the metric system on its missions while Lockheed Martin, the contractor who built the MCO, conducted its operations with the English system of measurement. When the NASA engineers attempted to correct the course of the MCO, the ground computers showed different coordinates than the satellite.[7]

How could NASA have made such a basic mistake with one of their most important programs? The short answer is they did not communicate their expectations effectively. NASA had been using the metric system[8] as their primary measurement system since 1990, meaning this was not a recent change or their first mission under these constraints. NASA failed in relaying to their contractor what they needed their equipment to do; they assumed their measurement requirements were obvious.[9]

It's the responsibility of a leader to ensure the expectations are clear to everyone within their organization or a project. Those in charge should never assume their people inherently understand what performance goals are desired from them. Explicit rules and standards allow people to produce exactly what their leadership is looking for. As leaders implement this direct line of communication, they improve the efficiency of their organization.

MISSION FIRST, PEOPLE ALWAYS

Raising the Bar

An example of proper communication of expectations lies in the 2005 sports drama *Coach Carter*, which recounts the true story of Ken Carter, a man who returned to his former school to lead the basketball team. When Coach Carter arrives, he finds the current players are talented but lack respect and discipline. He immediately lays out his expectations for his new players, which stands in stark contrast to what they are familiar with. He gives his players individual contracts which state that, if they want to be members of his team, they must agree to not just attend all their classes but to sit in the front row. They are also required to wear dress shirts and ties on game days, refer to everyone on the team (player and coach alike) as "sir," and maintain a C+ grade point average.

At first, the players think these standards are laughable; they have never had rules and restrictions placed on them to play basketball. There is instant backlash with the two top scorers immediately quitting. They believe their talent puts them above those kinds of expectations.

The remaining team members sign the contracts and become successful under Coach Carter's expectations. They even find themselves in the middle of an undefeated season for the first time in the school's history – until Carter receives less-than-satisfactory progress reports. He forfeits each upcoming game until the team raises its average academic performance.

Instead of letting this tear them apart, the Richmond High School players rally and decide not to blame the coach for them not meeting his expectations but to put in the necessary work. Even when the school forces Carter to open the gym for practices and games, the players refuse to participate until they better their grades.[10]

Leaders who set clear, detailed expectations for their teams can uphold those standards. As those in leadership roles plainly explain what they expect and how to achieve these objectives, processes become much smoother for everyone.

Share Organizational Goals

Without goals, we are like ships without a destination, aimlessly floating through the sea. For an organization to gain needed direction, everything starts with a leader. Those who are transparent about their production objectives give their people something to look forward to and guide them in their daily actions.

Unorganized Labor

Superstore, a TV series that began in 2015, follows a wayward millennial named Jonah, who dropped out of business school and applied at the first place he found that was hiring: a chain department store called Cloud 9. The show revolves around Jonah; Amy, the floor manager; and a group of well-meaning but ridiculous employees as they go through the daily drudge of working at a "superstore."

In the season one finale, the store manager Glenn is fired for going against company policy by granting an employee maternity leave. Upon learning this, Jonah and Amy fight the injustice by spreading the news to their coworkers and organizing a walkout. The episode closes with a dramatic shot of employees exiting the store.[11]

The next season begins with everyone standing in the parking lot, the ultimate destination of their walkout. They appear less sure of themselves as they glance at Jonah and Amy. Everyone has taken a big risk in leaving their jobs with no security. Someone eventually asks the question that is on everyone's mind: "What now?"

Without a goal to focus their efforts, the initial zeal that drove everyone to vacate Cloud 9 quickly fades. Jonah and Amy try to hold onto their people with fiery rhetoric, but the employees question why they actually took the risk of leaving in the first place. Slowly but surely, the strike dwindles down to Jonah and Amy, the last two holdouts of the dramatic exodus.[12]

From this example, it's clear that communicated goals help people focus their efforts on what's important for the success of their organization as well as themselves. As leaders develop these targets, they deliver a vision of shared triumph that can be achieved with proper direction. Individuals can also be inspired by working toward these larger objectives as opposed to their monotonous day-to-day tasks. Those holding leadership roles must be able to truly convey these intentions in a clear and understandable way to gain support from within their organization.

"I Have a Dream."

We've seen this before in the Civil Rights Movement of the 1950s as it spread across the country advocating for vague and inconsistent end goals. Dr. Martin Luther King Jr. first came onto the scene when he was chosen as the official leader and spokesmen for the Montgomery Bus Boycott in 1955. Soon after, he founded the Southern Leadership Christian Conference (SCLC), whose motto was: "Not one hair of one head of one person should be harmed."[13]

It was under his leadership that the organization was able to make its largest impact. Dr. King traveled across the country and the world, lecturing on the benefits of nonviolent protests and civil rights. Using this platform, he unified the crusade under one, clear message and made sure everyone knew what that was. The goals of that movement came to a pinnacle in his famous "I Have a Dream" speech where he said the following:

> There are those who are asking the devotees of civil rights, "When will you be satisfied?" We can never be satisfied as long as the Negro is the victim of the unspeakable horrors of police brutality. We can never be satisfied as long as our bodies, heavy with the fatigue of travel, cannot gain lodging in the motels of the highways and the hotels of the cities.

> We cannot be satisfied as long as the negro's basic mobility is from a smaller ghetto to a larger one. We can never be satisfied as long as our children are stripped of

their self-hood and robbed of their dignity by signs stating: "For Whites Only."

We cannot be satisfied as long as a Negro in Mississippi cannot vote, and a Negro in New York believes he has nothing for which to vote.
I have a dream that my four little children will one day live in a nation where they will not be judged by the color of their skin, but by the content of their character.[14]

As the leader of the Civil Rights Movement during the fifties and sixties, Dr. King was one of the great communicators of the modern era as he informed the world of the social demonstration's objective. Putting a voice and a face to the goals of the crusade inspired an entire generation and helped them to accomplish feats that have had a lasting effect.

Being open with your people will not only make them respect you more, but will push them to work toward that common objective. If employees are kept in the dark, they blindly follow their leader with no attachment to a positive outcome as opposed to marching on together toward a shared goal. As leaders trust their people with plans and the overall success of the business, they create opportunities for everyone to rally around.

Share Organizational Success

Success is one of the greatest cures for many issues that plague any group. It lifts people up and gives them confidence in the work they're doing. Organizations that are unsuccessful suffer over time from a decline of morale in those within. It's the responsibility of a leader to highlight and commend the victories, big and small, of their team. When leaders share their wins, it not only serves as a standard for their own people, but as a message to those outside of their organization.

MISSION FIRST, PEOPLE ALWAYS

"We Shall Go on to the End."

Winston Churchill stepped into leadership of the English government in 1940 as Adolf Hitler began his conquest of the European continent. Prime Minister Churchill was trusted to stand up to Hitler and his Nazi regime, who was achieving success unlike anything Europe had seen since Napoleon. This terrified British citizens, as they saw themselves as the dictator's next destination with France's defeat looming in the imminent future. Prime Minister Churchill made the pointed decision to reverse course from his predecessor and take an aggressive approach to combat the German forces sweeping over Europe.

England sent 300,000-plus troops over the English Channel to France and Belgium to assist them in staving off the German onslaught. Unfortunately, the Allied Forces underestimated the ferocity and efficiency of the German's *blitzkrieg* and were pushed to the shores of Dunkirk. As they waited for the Germans to finish them off, Prime Minister Churchill demanded "Operation Dynamo" be put into effect.

This operation involved the English government enlisting every seaworthy vessel available – civilian and military alike – to sail to Dunkirk as quickly as possible and begin an immediate emergency evacuation. Despite moving with a speed seldom seen in government planning, the prime minister remained distressed. He believed the Germans would bombard the immobile armies; they would be lucky if they rescued 10% of their men. In what has since come to be known as the "Dunkirk Miracle," the Royal Air Force was able to hold off the German attack long enough for nearly all British forces to be evacuated safely. After the successful evacuation, Prime Minister Churchill spoke to the people of his country not about the major defeat in battle they had just suffered, but the victory of Operation Dynamo.[15]

Before the House of Commons, Churchill remarked on the evacuation of Dunkirk, saying:

> The Royal Navy, with the willing help of countless merchant seamen, strained every nerve to embark the British and Allied troops; 220 light warships and 650 other

vessels were engaged. They had to operate upon the difficult coast, often in adverse weather, under a ceaseless hail of bombs and an increasing concentration of artillery fire. Nor were the seas, as I have said, themselves free from mines and torpedoes. It was in conditions such as these that our men carried on, with little or no rest, for days and nights on end, making trip after trip...

A miracle of deliverance, achieved by valor, by perseverance, by perfect discipline, by faultless service, by resource, by skill, by unconquerable fidelity, is manifest to us all. The enemy was hurled back by the retreating British and French troops. He was so roughly handled that he did not hurry their departure seriously. The Royal Air Force engaged the main strength of the German Air Force, and inflicted upon them losses of at least four to one; and the Navy, using nearly 1,000 ships of all kinds, carried over 335,000 men, French and British, out of the jaws of death and shame, to their native land and to the tasks which lie immediately ahead.

This was a great trial of strength between the British and German Air Forces. Can you conceive a greater objective for the Germans in the air than to make evacuation from these beaches impossible, and to sink all these ships which were displayed, almost to the extent of thousands? Could there have been an objective of greater military importance and significance for the whole purpose of the war than this?[16]

The prime minister's words brought hope to the English people and inspired them to find the courage to continue to fend off Hitler's forces. This was a particularly vulnerable time, for some leaders in the British government had suggested they attempt some form of appeasement in the face of daunting odds. If Prime Minister Churchill had focused his message on the major defeat instead of the miraculous evacuation, it might've been enough to break the will of his people and colleagues. His ability to motivate and impress the British residents allowed him to lead the nation to triumph in one of the most significant wars in the world.

Leaders perform little labor accomplished by an organization: generals do not fight battles, coaches do not play in games, and managers are not usually the ones accomplishing the ground-level work. This makes it even more important that they effectively communicate why their people should perform their duties to the best of their abilities. People in power are excited to show their people what they can accomplish by sharing successes; and, if they can see what already has been achieved, they'll most likely find their own path forward easier.

Share Organizational Needs

The distribution of the organization's needs is an important responsibility that many leaders neglect because they do not recognize its necessity. They may misunderstand the benefit in telling those above them what they're lacking and view it as admitting defeat in some way, but this couldn't be further from the truth. Leaders who identify issues and ask for help or resources with their higher-ups will set themselves and their team up for success.

The prioritization of their people's needs is essential as well. This selflessness as a leader enables their organization to work without the worry of being hindered by unnecessary problems, such as a deficit in assets.

Creating a culture of sharing the needs of your organization can be difficult. This is especially true in a military environment where the mindset is that the presence of any weakness can be perceived as failure. I have watched several supervisors fail or produce substandard work rather than admit they needed more assistance. Leaders who cannot overcome their own pride to ask for support will put the success and the wellbeing of their people in danger.

Communication

Saving Face

About a year into my time at Luke AFB, Captain Samuels arrived at the 56th Maintenance Group to take command of one of the AMUs. Having recently dealt with the bureaucracy of in-processing at Luke, I showed him around and helped him settle into his new position. While talking, I discovered he had taken an untraditional career path, undertaking mostly administrative positions until that point. He felt nervous to be in his first leadership role so late in his career. He was years behind his peers in terms of his development as a maintenance officer and felt pressure not to reveal any incompetence or uncertainty to others.

This became evident in the way he conducted himself in group production meetings. No matter how dire the circumstances seemed to be, he refused to voice concerns. Other officers responsible for AMUs, myself included, requested extra airmen or additional resources from the maintenance group during one meeting when we underwent a time of being particularly low on operational aircraft. Capt. Samuels and his team pressed through whatever adversity came their way. They eventually rebounded without help from any outside organization.

I was rather impressed by this at the time, and I respected how Capt. Samuels and his team seemed to succeed where it seemed mine had come up short. That was until I talked to one of my former NCOs who had transferred into Capt. Samuel's AMU. He explained how the morale of the AMU was one of the lowest he'd ever seen. When maintainers brought issues to leadership, their concerns were dismissed, or they were told to find ways around them. The leadership – from the AMU superintendent all the way down to shift supervisors – had adopted Capt. Samuel's mentality to not admit inadequacies within the unit. Airmen were required to continually work long, grueling shifts and weekends just to hit the minimum requirements to remain operational. This didn't solve the problems in their department; it only hid them as they grew and hurt his people in the end.

Effective leaders understand their purpose is to help their team become successful and maintain productivity versus obtaining glory for themselves. These two things are not always mutually exclusive; organizational success often comes with plenty of credit for the leader. However, if a choice must be made between the two, it's the job of the leader to elevate and share issues within the organization to ensure they are properly dealt with. Those who adhere to that principle will save their people unnecessary suffering.

The Jewish Queen of Persia

The Bible tells the story of the courageous leadership of Esther, Queen of Persia, which was one of the most powerful empires of its time. Esther was of Jewish descent; her people had been brought captive into Babylon following the fall of Jerusalem in 600 B.C. Orphaned as a young girl, Esther was raised in Babylon by her older cousin, Mordecai, who brought her up in the Jewish faith and taught her to honor the customs of her people.

When the King of Persia announced he was searching for a new queen, Mordecai presented Esther, known for her beauty, for consideration. Upon meeting the woman, the patriarch felt there was something special about her, something that set her apart from the other beautiful maidens he had met. So, having gained the king's favor, Esther was selected out of many women to become queen. Even after marrying, she kept her identity as a Jew secret from everyone in the royal court.

Soon after Esther stepped into her role, she faced a crisis. Haman, an advisor to the king, proposed a royal decree that declared all Jews within the Persian Empire to be killed. It was a personal vendetta, for Haman hated the Jews and saw them as arrogant and insubordinate for refusing to bow before him. He persuaded the ruler, telling him that the Jews could not be trusted to be loyal to the Persian because of their devotion to God. The king agreed and unwittingly ordered the death of his new queen.

Communication

This royal order placed Esther in a difficult position. She could continue to keep her identity hidden and live in luxury as queen, or she could utilize the full influence of her position by sharing the plight of her people. Up to this point in Persia, the queen's role had been primarily ornamental; Esther was responsible for pleasing the king and bearing heirs. By going before the ruler and representing the struggles of the Jews, she would not just jeopardize her position as queen but her life.

Esther ultimately decided she had a duty to come forward and plead the case of the Jews. Before going to the king, she sent Mordecai to instruct her people to fast and pray on her behalf as recorded in the Book of Esther 4:16: "Go, gather together all the Jews that are present in Shushan, and fast ye for me, and neither eat nor drink three days, night or day: I also and my maidens will fast likewise; and so will I go in unto the king, which is not according to the law: and if I perish, I perish."

Esther's courage was rewarded as the king reversed his decree. Going one step further, the patriarch ordered a new injunction that granted the Jewish people protection throughout the land from any who would wish to harm them. The leadership shown by Esther in communicating the needs of her people saved thousands from slaughter and set them up to become a great nation.

Leaders who fail to identify and discuss the needs of their people are individuals who care about their short-term reputations more than the long-term successes of their organizations and teams. To successfully guide anyone, those in leadership must provide their people with the resources needed to succeed. They must overcome fear and pride in order to communicate effectively to higher-ups, who can make assets and training readily available. A person attempting to lead without this skill will cripple the potential of an organization.

Communication Reflection Questions

- When is the last time you had a formal feedback session with one of your people? Who was it and how did it go?
- Who's been doing a good job recently that you should give feedback to? What do you plan to say?
- Now, who needs to improve in your organization? What do they need to do in order to better themselves and achieve personal and/or career objectives?

Setting Clear Expectations

- What does the word "expectation" mean to you?
- What specific expectations do you have for those in your organization? Have you shared these with them?
- What are standards your people can expect you to meet?

Share Organizational Goals

- What are your short-term goals for your organization?
- How about your long-term goals?

Share Organizational Success

- What are some successes your organization has accomplished recently?
- Does *your* leadership know about the wins your organization has achieved?

Share Organizational Needs

- Does your organization need anything to be more successful? If so, what is it?
- Who's the person that can help you meet these needs?
- Are they aware of these requirements necessary to your people? If not, why is that?

2

DELEGATION

Before being commissioned as officers in the Air Force, all ROTC cadets must attend field training. This is a leadership course with physical and mental challenges meant to place aspiring officers under continual stress. It's in these taxing situations that the certified training assistants (CTAs) test leadership and decision-making abilities; they, along with assigned officers, evaluate which individuals have what it takes to be in the Air Force and which ones do not.

Everything done at field training – from how meals are eaten to the time it takes to get dressed – has to meet or exceed the standards of the CTAs assigned to the flight. The guiding philosophy behind all of this is to see who will break under the pressure over the next month. It's thought that a person who can't handle manufactured stress will not be able to handle real-world hardships, especially when that individual is counted on to make decisions that affect the lives of others.

During this course, I participated in a series of group leadership projects (GLPs). These are timed obstacle courses that involve problem-solving tests meant to be completed as a team. There are many unique solutions that could be used to overcome the presented challenges. Teams of cadets, with one person designated as the leader, were directed to collaborate, create, and implement a solution within 15 minutes.

I was selected as my team's leader. As we entered the GLP course, I went to receive the instructions for the parameters our team would have to operate within and listened intently to our CTA as he detailed the rules for this particular course. By the time he had told me what my rules of engagement were and what resources we had access to, I had already brainstormed several ideas. The clock started, and I explained the rules to my team and discussed the potential solutions with which I'd come up. After hearing their input, we agreed on our methods. I placed our supplies to build our path and, once it was finished, I demonstrated how to traverse it effectively. I cheered on each of my team members as they made it through the end.

Having completed the course in a timely manner with my team, I expected high praise as I received my evaluation. I earned great scores for course completion, but my overall leadership scores were low. The two deductions I remember the most were (1) not utilizing the strengths of my team and (2) organizing everything myself. My CTA explained that, as a leader, even if you can complete a task single-handedly, it's more important to understand how to delegate tasks. In doing so, the GLP would've allowed me to step back and involve everyone as well as spot potential problems that might occur as they designed the path. I was so fixated on completing the course that I faltered on leading my team.

Delegation is one of the skills most inherently tied to leadership. Leaders are expected to give tasks out to those they supervise. What separates someone who is just a boss and a two-part leader is how they delegate. Two-part leaders must delegate work to their people with deliberate purpose. They cannot throw out tasks to their team haphazardly and without thought. Doing so wastes the opportunity to build their people and create a more effective organization.

Focus on Leading

Today, leadership is seen as more of a personality trait than a necessary skill for those in positions of power; it's often not emphasized as something that needs to be honed as much as other technical abilities. Effective and matured leadership adds value and maintains order within an organization and in individual teams. While leaders may possess other skills that could be used, their leadership provides the most impact.

There's a difference between the roles of officers and enlisted members in the ranks of the U.S. military. That distinction boils down to area of expertise and scope of responsibility. Enlisted members are considered technical experts; their jobs are to answer possible questions within their particular field. Officers, however, are trained to lead before anything else. They have specialty career fields they are placed in and prepared for, but that's still secondary to their role as leaders.

Understanding Your Role

Before I began my career as a maintenance officer, I attended the Aircraft Maintenance Officer's Course (AMOC), training that illustrated, through aircraft operations, how the supply system worked and what the responsibilities were of each organization within a maintenance group. The course contained enough information for me to understand how all the aspects of my career field worked in conjunction, though not enough to be a specialist on any one part. The Air Force didn't expect me to become subject matter authority – they wanted me to become an expert in how to lead.

I marveled every day at the work my maintainers in the 309th AMU completed on the flight line. Each night, we had malfunctioning fighter jets return after having been pushed to their limits. My airmen used their system knowledge to diagnose and fix issues, usually all within the span of a single eight-hour shift. If I were to go out there and help them turn wrenches, it wouldn't have been beneficial. The way I added value to the organization was through leading; I represented their successes and needs in meetings with the group commander, ensuring they got the support they required to perform.

Good leaders are those who want to help their organization at any cost. It's important for these leaders to realize that the best way for them to help their people is through leading as opposed to taking on minor tasks. Focusing on delegation and guidance allows those in charge to allocate their full attention to making the right decisions for their people.

Lawn-Chair Leadership

The 2008 film *Forever Strong* is based on the life of Rick Penning, an out-of-control high school rugby star who found himself at his lowest point when he ended up in juvenile detention after getting into a car accident that was the result of his drunk driving. While in custody, one of the counselors noticed Rick's natural athletic ability and presented the teen with an interesting offer: he would be given the option to play rugby for Highland High, the local high school and the rival of his former team, through an outreach program.

At the time, Highland High was the most prominent rugby team in the country at that age group. Under Coach Larry Gelwix, Highland Rugby achieved an amazing 418-10 record and won 20 national championships. Rick initially bristled at the idea of playing for Highland High School. Despite his first reaction, his curiosity eventually triumphed.[17]

Rick was shocked by his first week of practice; the assistant coaches ran the drills and taught the actual technique while Coach Gelwix sat in his lawn chair. Rick voiced his displeasure to his new teammates of what he perceived as the coach's lack of interest in their development as players. He was immediately spurned by players who had been on the team for years; they insisted he had a reason for everything he did.

Soon, it became obvious that there were many people who could runs drills or teach technique. What made Highland the best was the leadership of Coach Gelwix, who was able to observe his players' strengths, weaknesses, and where they best fit into the team. He implemented game strategies that showcased the strengths of his players to attack the weaknesses of the opposing teams.[18] This leadership included more than just game strategy; he understood his players and what they needed to reach their potential on and off the field.

Delegation

It can be difficult for leaders to step back from the daily duties of their organization. Taking time to focus on larger issues and decisions can feel like they're somehow not putting in their fair share of work. What individuals who are new to positions of leadership need to realize is that the way to best assist their people is by concentrating on making proper decisions on behalf of their team. The more effective leadership one can bring to their organization, the more productive they will become.

Prioritize Your Work

As a leader, one of the first steps of proper delegation is determining what work has to be done by you and what can be done by others. Those who are unable to draw this distinction risk putting their organizations in dangerous situations, such as missing vital assignments because they got caught up in work that could have easily been performed by someone else. It's a necessity to make these choices as a leader takes over a new position. You have to know what work you're responsible for and prioritize it while sharing other chores with people skilled in those areas.

Forming a Functional Team

When I was a newly promoted captain, I also took on the position of risk manager for a new Air Force weapons system. My team and I were responsible for creating the processes to oversee all risks, issues, and concerns connected to our program's $9 billion contract. My mind raced when I learned I'd be stepping into this role: I ruminated about the elements that would go into establishing a new risk management program and planned how I'd get them all done. It took me less than an hour to realize that if I did not delegate work to my team members, I wouldn't be able to give adequate attention to the most important aspects of the new process.

MISSION FIRST, PEOPLE ALWAYS

In our first meeting, I laid the foundation for the prioritization of work going forward by gathering information on my employees' strengths. Together, we outlined every assignment, meeting, and deliverable required of the program risk team to have the impact we wanted. I identified the tasks that my leaders mandated me a part of as well as what I felt was important for me to do to maintain control of the team's direction. With everything in place, I devoted myself to high-profile events, such as quarterly risk reviews with the contractor, working with the team leads to communicate their prospects to leadership, and updating government documents. These were things only I could do because of my position.

Delegating other responsibilities did more than just free my time to focus on the essential tasks; in fact, it allowed the members of my team to carve out what roles they wanted. Instead of merely assisting me, they were given specific responsibilities and processes they could own. I appointed one of my team members as the head of risk management training and development. Another person became the risk inventory manger. They grew from the shared responsibility and agency their new roles gave them.

Leaders must understand the significance of delegation and force themselves to do so for their less impactful work. Many newcomers to leadership roles struggle with this concept, for they want to have their finger on everything that goes on within their organization. While the choices surrounding who gets which responsibilities can be complex, leaders risk jeopardizing their more important work or burning themselves out if they cannot distribute work to others. This, regrettably, is a lesson that some learn the hard way.

They Shall Bear the Burden with Thee

The Book of Exodus describes the story of the prophet Moses liberating the Hebrews from bondage. He performed great miracles to convince the pharaoh to release the Hebrews from slavery, including parting the Red Sea. After winning his people's freedom, Moses led them through the wilderness in search of the

Delegation

Promised Land. This was a joyous time for the Israelites after being in captivity for over 400 years, though they experienced much strife; for the first time in generations, they were responsible for governing themselves.

During this period, Moses was visited by his father-in-law Jethro who supported him in his relatively new role as a prophet and a leader. Jethro observed that Moses spent most of his day sitting in judgment, ruling on trivial matters. Understanding the heavy burden Moses carried, Jethro counseled him to delegate some of his burden to allow him to better lead his people in Exodus 18:17-22:

> Moses' father-in-law said unto him, "The thing that thou doest is not good. Thou wilt surely wear away, both thou and this people that is with thee: for this thing is too heavy for thee; thou art not able to perform it thyself alone. Hearken now unto my voice, I will give thee counsel, and God shall be with thee: Be thou for the people to Godward, that thou mayest bring the causes unto God: And thou shalt teach them ordinances and laws, and shalt shew them the way wherein they must walk, and the work that they must do.
>
> Moreover, thou shalt provide out of all the people able men, such as fear God, men of truth, hating covetousness; and place such over them, to be rulers of thousands, and rulers of hundreds, rulers of fifties, and rulers of tens: And let them judge the people at all seasons: and it shall be, that every great matter they shall bring unto thee, but every small matter they shall judge: so shall it be easier for thyself, and they shall bear the burden with thee."

Jethro understood that Moses had more important things to do for his people than sit in judgment all day. He was a spiritual leader for his people. The Israelites looked to Moses to bring them God's instructions on how they were to live their everyday lives and, on top of that, he was responsible for leading approximately 2 million people through the desert to the Promised Land. By adhering to Jethro's advice and appointing judges to deal with smaller matters, Moses freed himself to be a more focused leader.

Every individual in charge must, at some point, make these choices for themselves. Sometimes recognizing what is vital for leadership to take care of will be obvious while other instances will be ambiguous. Most importantly is the need for delegation which will teach you how to process these decisions faster and more effectively.

Recognize the Strengths of Your People

To be able to delegate effectively, a leader must identify both the strengths and weaknesses of their people. The distribution of tasks is not random. Rather, it needs to be a thoughtful process where duties are given to those who are familiar with what's being asked of them and who will be able to do the best for their organization.

The Great War Against Buggers

In the 1985 science fiction novel *Ender's Game,* Orson Scott Card illustrates how a leader can confidently entrust certain tasks to their people to operate at maximum efficiency. The book is set in a reality where Earth is preparing to fend off invaders called Buggers yet again. As part of this preparation, the world's most intelligent children are sent to a military academy called Battle School, where they train to be future military leaders; one of these kids is Andrew "Ender" Wiggin. In Battle School, students are pitted against each other in war scenarios that has them act as both soldiers and commanders. Ender is chosen from his peers at the young age of five as the Earth's best hope against the Buggers.

Since Ender has been identified as the last chance to save the world, he is tested and trained beyond the normal level for a student in the program. He consistently faces seemingly no-win situations where he creates his own advantages. Ender overcomes staggering odds again and again due to superior strategy and finding value in those people who others have given up on.

Delegation

During his time at the Battle School, Ender becomes the greatest commander that they ever trained.

When Ender is deemed ready to command the entire fleet in the war against the Buggers, he believes he is embarking on one final test, one last game. In the computer simulation, he commands his fleet against the enemy which greatly outnumbers him. His closest Battle School comrades are allowed to participate as his squadron commanders prepare to obey his every order. Ender, knowing the strengths each of his leaders brings to the battlefield, utilizes them to create a seamless attack.

> They learned many ways of working together, as the simulator forced them to try different situations. Sometimes the simulator gave them a larger fleet to work with; Ender set them up then in three or four toons that consisted of three or four squadrons each. Sometimes the simulator gave them a single starship with its twelve fighters, and he chose three squadron leaders with four fighters each.
>
> It was pleasure; it was play… In the three weeks they practiced together, Ender came to know them very well. Dink, who deftly carried out instructions but was slow to improvise; Bean, who couldn't control large groups of ships effectively but could use only a few like a scalpel, reacting beautifully to anything the computer threw at him; Alai, who was almost as good a strategist as Ender and could be entrusted to do well with half a fleet and only vague instructions…[19]

Ender designates his people like this because he knows their skillsets. As Ender's trust in his comrades is repeatedly rewarded within the simulation, it helps them work seamlessly together.

Delegating people based on their capabilities not only streamlines production, but builds trust within that group. Leaders must demonstrate the thought and effort that goes into their team assignments instead of haphazardly pushing work off onto the first person they think of. Operating this way will take more initial exertion on the leader's behalf to observe and understand the strengths of each of individual, but that will pay off in the long run. This allows leaders to simultaneously develop their cohort and reduce the inefficiency.

Make Clear Assignments

Not clarifying assignments unnecessarily compounds the already difficult habit of delegation. Whenever a supervisor distributes work to those in their organization, they do so in an effort to ensure the work is completed. Vague directions only frustrate leaders when their vision is not carried out how they imagined. There are few things more stressful to an individual than knowing their boss wants them to finish a task without having explicit expectations attached to said assignment.

Napoleon Bonaparte – known still as one of the most successful and genius generals in global military history – always broke down his commands to their most basic parts. He observed that "any order that can be misunderstood will be misunderstood."[20] He acknowledged how even brilliant leaders cannot be effective if they can't get their people to comprehend what they're supposed to do.

"There's Always Money in the Banana Stand."

A great example of this can be found in the comedy show *Arrested Development*, which grew a cult following after it was aired from 2003-2006. The series centers on the Bluths, a greedy and self-centered family at the head of a major real estate company. George Bluth, the patriarchal head, is first shown in prison, awaiting his trial for embezzling funds from his own business. During one of his visits, George's son, Michael, reviews his father's defense strategy while worrying aloud about the increasing cost of the legal fees. George reassures his son by leaning over and winking at Michael before saying, "There's always money in the banana stand."

Delegation

The Bluth Frozen Banana Stand, which the family has owned for decades, is located on the Newport Beach Pier. Even though their real estate company faltered, their shop continues to sell frozen fruit to beach-goers year in and year out. Michael understands his father's comment as a suggestion to invest more time into the basics of their business; he spends an increasing amount of time trying to expand the banana stand while managing the real estate company. He even requires his own son to work long, taxing hours at the banana stand, exhausting every resource to make money.

Michael's focus on work and money eventually strains his relationship with his son. He has an epiphany: the only thing that could come from his efforts would be a family that resents him. In a unifying and cathartic moment, Michael and his son burn down the frozen fruit stand, realizing that family is most important.

When Michael shares this experience with George in his next visit to the prison, he provokes a stronger reaction than expected: George screams, "There was $250,000 lining the walls of the banana stand. How much clear can I say 'There's money in the banana stand?'"[21]

As imperfect human beings, our thoughts seem to make sense to ourselves and it's sometimes challenging to get others to understand concepts the way we do. For a leader to delegate, it is essential to communicate assignments and responsibilities in a way that others understand. A leader cannot effectively entrust work if they over-explain and confuse people or under-explain and omit important details.

They Hadn't Advertised – at All

Another instance in which unclear instructions made a task more painful than it needed to be was when I was a brand-new flight commander. I'd been given the task of becoming the squadron's representative for the Combined Federal Campaign (CFC), the charitable arm of the federal government which lists hundreds of charities for a variety of causes that Air Force members can contribute to. The CFC accepts donations year-round, but makes a month-long push every spring where they get most of their subsidies.

My responsibility as CFC rep was to advertise and collect donations during that month. The AFB had an overall goal for the amount of money they wanted to raise, which worked its way down to each squadron having a specific goal. I enlisted the help of a SNCO in each flight to help me manage the program, and I counted on them to manage the CFC within their limits and report back to me with results.

When it came time for each flight's first progress report, I found myself frustrated at the low numbers. It was agitating to discover that most of my flight reps hadn't advertised the CFC at all. I complained to my flight chief that I was ready to fire them and undertake the whole endeavor myself. He asked to see the email traffic between me and the designated reps in each of the flights and proceeded to scour them. As he wrapped up, he turned to me and taught me an especially important lesson in delegation.

He explained that my emails only detailed the results I wanted versus methods to achieve them. I'd asked my flight reps to advertise and help raise money for the CFC, but did not explain to them how I wanted it done. My flight chief then listed the following to hold people accountable and allow them to meet expectations:

1. Whenever a leader delegates, they need to understand that, most of the time, their people are not privy to the big picture. Thus, it's helpful for them to receive more context.
2. It's important to tell them what the results should look like. This is not the entire message, but it is an important piece.
3. Once they have an idea what needs to be done, a leader should then describe how to do it. Those in charge should ask themselves the question: "Are there any milestones along the way that need to be explained?" and give more information about this if the answer is "Yes."

4. A leader needs to specify what level of quality is expected. For example, if a PowerPoint is assigned, is it purely informational for the team or to exhibit before an executive?
5. Team members should be aware of how long they have to work on a project. Without any kind of deadline given, these tasks will not be prioritized, and assignments can fall to the wayside.

Thanks to the assistance and wisdom of my flight chief, I was able to course-correct and let my flight reps know clearly what I expected of them. This experience taught me that, when people do not meet my expectations, instead of blaming them outright, I need to self-reflect and see if *I* failed *them*. Delegation is an important tool for a leader, though it can unravel their plans if not used properly.

Empower Your People

Trust is of the utmost importance when a leader gives a task to someone in their organization because they have to believe in their colleague enough to allow them autonomy over their assignment. It is more work to delegate an activity to someone and constantly look over their shoulder to make sure they do things exactly the way you would've – and no one likes a leader who micromanages. Effective delegation means you give your people the authority and latitude to perform their specified duties and match your expectations. The more independence leaders grant those they supervise in undertaking and completing projects, the more creative problem-solving there will be.

Edison vs. Tesla

Thomas Edison is known as one of the greatest inventors in American history for his invention of the lightbulb, phonograph, and of the technology for motion pictures. These creations helped Edison establish the international manufacturing company Edison General Electric, where he employed many bright engineers and scientists. One noteworthy scientist was Nikola Tesla.

Tesla – who studied physics, mathematics, and mechanics at the Austrian Polytechnic School – proved himself to be a diamond in the rough while working for Edison. He saved the company from embarrassment and financial loss by improving existing electrical systems installed in both Germany and America. Tesla accomplished what other engineers couldn't, thanks to his ability to decipher complicated problems before even seeing any of the equipment in person.

Before he worked for Edison, Tesla developed a theory that would later go on to change the world: alternating current (AC). AC was cheaper, could travel longer distances, and was overall more efficient than direct current (DC), which was the primary method electricity was utilized in that period. Edison recognized Tesla's emerging talent. Despite this, when Tesla presented his theory and explained how it could revolutionize Edison's company, Edison responded, "Spare me that nonsense. It's dangerous. We're set up for direct current in America. People like it, and it's all I'll ever fool with."[22] In other words, he meant, "I come up with the ideas and you'll carry out my instructions."

Soon after his idea was dismissed by the renowned inventor, Tesla quit Edison General Electric and joined Westinghouse Electric Company, which – with Telsa's help – won the highly-contested bid to provide the power for the Chicago World's Fair using AC electricity. This loss dealt a huge blow to Edison and DC electricity; both became viewed as limited and obsolete by the world.[23]

Although Edison was a brilliant inventor, he stifled creativity in others by not empowering them. When a leader does not support and encourage their people, they limit their organization's capacity for innovation and problem-solving to one person's ideas. That hierarchal thinking often ruins those in leadership roles when they can't let go of their ego. Such indifference to others' input causes those in a position of power to lose the effectiveness that comes with delegation.

Delegation

The Universal Ruler

Temujin Borjigin worked his way from slavery to one of the most known (and feared) leaders in the world. Through military and political genius, he was able to bring all Mongolian tribes under one banner for the first time in the country's history – after which, he was given the title Genghis Khan, which translates as "the universal ruler." Over the next 20 years, he assembled and wielded one of the most successful military campaigns in recorded history.

By the time he died, Genghis Khan had conquered over 9 million square miles (over twice the size of modern-day China) and ruled 25% of the world's population under his empire. The Mongolian khan's reign stretched from northeastern Russia to eastern Europe and reached as far as the Middle East and even Japan.[24] In the lands he obtained, he established a common law known as *Yassa*, which prohibited adultery, theft, blood feuds, and religious persecution. Unbeknownst to many, he also adopted those he defeated as Mongol citizens and allowed them to rise to positions of prominence instead of enslaving them.[25]

To manage an army and empire of such magnitude, Genghis Khan empowered those in his organization and trusted them with important decisions. He supplied his top generals power to spearhead independent campaigns. The conqueror's troops were divvied into groups of *arban* (10), *zegun* (100), *mingan* (1,000), and *tumen* (10,000). Each *arban*, *zegun*, and *mingan* within Khan's army selected their own leader to represent and guide them into battle.[24]

As a great military and civic leader, Genghis Khan understood the significance of investing in the abilities of his people and enabling them to lead their own cohorts. He knew everyone possessed valuable perspectives on what would help them succeed. By empowering individuals to make decisions pertaining to military operations, he secured their loyalty. Once people feel they have a say within an organization, they are more attached to its success.

Don't Overload Your People

It's worth repeating: a leader should avoid taking on too much of their organization's work. In the same vein, however, it is vital they do not place too much on those in their employ. This might seem obvious, but it's an easy mistake to make, especially with individuals who seem like they can excel at any task thrown their way. You must pay attention to this delicate balance in order to maintain an efficient unit.

Spreading the Wealth

I learned how to spread out my responsibilities and not overload myself nor people in my organization from observing my maintenance group commander Colonel Anderson. Each AMU at Luke AFB was tasked with the training and progression of either F-16 or F-35 student pilots. Occasionally, the AFB would get a request to use our aircraft in support of another base with an exercise or operation they had going on, which meant one of the AMUs was required to prepare twice as many aircraft as they normally would. There were times that, due to manpower constraints, the AMU could not supply this amount. Officers in charge (OICs) did not want to admit to not having the necessary personnel and let the maintenance group commander down by not meeting mission requirements.

If an AMU was unable to supply the needed number of aircraft, it showed during the production meeting. Col. Anderson would review the previous day's reports and notice the AMU had not filled all the flight slots they had scheduled. Instead of laying into the officers and ordering them to manage their people and assets better, he would ask: "What do you need to get the job done?"

The problem often was solved right there. If an AMU was unable to provide the aircraft – whether for pilot training or extra assignments – Col. Anderson would search for and arrange for them to receive the necessary resources. He would borrow maintainers from another unit and loan them to the shorthanded unit, or he would tell a healthy AMU to fill some of the empty flying slots with their aircraft instead. Col. Anderson knew that if one of the AMUs under him crumbled under the pressure, the whole group would suffer.

Leaders must be aware of when to push their people and when to pull back because they've been overloaded. If a supervisor leans too hard on any one person, there's potential of that person breaking. However, if the person in charge recognizes this and fixes it in time, they can keep their organization functioning normally.

Burnout

Ricky Williams, a former college and NFL standout, was the kind of football player who comes around once in a generation. In a sport where everyone is a monstrous physical specimen, he stood out as a running back because of his combination of power and speed. He could as easily run around a tackler as he could run him over.

At the University of Texas, Ricky built a career where, in both his junior and senior seasons, he led the nation in rushing yards and touchdowns. In his senior year, he won the Heisman Trophy, naming him the best college football player in the country. When he left Texas, Ricky held or shared in 20 NCAA records.

Four years later, at 26 – an age still considered within an athlete's prime – Ricky retired from the sport. It's not uncommon for an athlete to retire early because of a debilitating injury, but, in this man's case, he simply got overused and burnt out. He said, "I led the NFL in attempts the last two years and they really didn't go out and get a quarterback to help me, so I knew it was going to be all on me again… It just became obvious to me that playing football for me is not going to be fun, not something I'm going to enjoy."[26]

Being overused was not the only factor that caused Ricky to leave the league, although it was the primary one. His coaches assumed his innate skills could carry the team without supplying help. Who knows the long and fruitful career Ricky Williams could've had if his needs had been met.

Once a leader finds that "go-to" person in their organization, it becomes easy to rely on them for everything they need without a second thought. But it is important to perceive the pressure they're putting on their people and whether it's too much for them to handle alone. All it takes is discipline to spread the load of work more evenly. Delegation, if utilized correctly, has the potential to let a leader focus on their main responsibilities, develop those in the organization, and maximize the work being done.

Delegation

Delegation Reflection Questions

- What value do you bring to your organization?
- How does your leadership allow your people do your job better?

Prioritize Your Work

- What is the work in the organization that *only* you can do?
- What work do you routinely delegate to others?
- If you are not currently delegating work, what are easy tasks you can start distributing?

Recognize the Strengths of Your People

- Who was the last person in your organization that you assigned a task or responsibility to?
- Why did you choose them for that responsibility?

Make Clear Assignments

- What was the last task you gave to someone on your team? Write down on scratch paper everything that assignment entailed.
- Did you give that person all the information they needed to be successful?
- What was the outcome of this duty? How, if at all, can you improve upon your current process to make it better in the future?

Empower Your People

- Do you expect your people to check in with you to complete their work?
- Does the work you assign your team members match the natural capabilities they have?

MISSION FIRST, PEOPLE ALWAYS

Don't Overload Your People

- ♣ Who is your "go-to person" in your organization? (Don't be shy; we all have one.)
- ♣ What do you do to ensure you don't overload them?
- ♣ How do you distribute the work throughout your organization? If you don't do this well already, how can you be better?

3

FOLLOW-UP

When I was a lieutenant in the 56th aircraft maintenance squadron (AMXS), we incorporated a continuous process improvement (CPI) program into all the AMUs. The program centered around the concept of removing waste from all daily processes we performed. Waste, in this context, means the misuse of manpower, resources, or time. Our squadron commander, Maj. Hanson, decided the CPI program was a perfect opportunity for the lieutenants to further practice their leadership skills by having them run it. Our assignment was to meet and update him weekly on what projects we were working on, how they were going to improve the AMU, and our progress.

The initial CPI meeting shocked us as we submitted our initial proposals and received rejections from Maj. Hanson. He chalked the proposals up to "busy-work projects" and that they wouldn't have a significant impact on the AMU's efficiency. He challenged us to look deeper at what our airmen required in order to work more productively when we reported to him the following week. We then understood these meetings would involve thorough and deliberate follow-up, not just a cursory interest at what we attempted to accomplish.

This caused me to shift my view from "what is a project I *could* do" to "what are projects I *should* do." I visited the flight line and observed specific processes the maintainers performed; everything from F-16 tire changing to how maintainers turned their tools in at the end of the day could be optimized. I created a way for airmen to communicate directly with leadership to let us know what procedures were broken and what resources they needed so we could adjust as necessary.

In our recurring meetings, Maj. Hanson pushed us to be specific with our status updates. What was our expected date of completion? Did we need any extra funds or further authorizations to move our projects forward? Not only had he demanded answers, but he also wanted to prove we knew what to do to better our AMUs.

Maj. Hanson following up on our projects and how we were progressing was instrumental in our success. The fact that he did not micromanage us and, instead, instilled agency within us to see what his vision was big for our overall development and motivation.

We have already learned how delegation is essential to leading a successful organization. Two-part leaders understand that following up is the oft-neglected other side of the delegation coin. Following up is a necessary tool for two-part leaders to properly vet the work, assignments, and programs they've distributed to their people. Properly following up can create teaching opportunities for leaders to help their people understand the importance of the work they are accomplishing and encourage their team to solve whatever issues they face the right way.

Assign Meaningful Work

Leaders delegate projects and assignments on a daily basis, which means it's important they dole out tasks worth doing, either for the progression of their overall organization's mission or for the development of their team. Verifying a task's purpose will save time and energy in the long run. Otherwise, supervisors will find themselves wasting resources following up on assignments of no consequence to them or their people.

The 440 Test

Syracuse University is a national powerhouse when it comes to men's collegiate lacrosse. Since NCAA lacrosse began in

Follow-Up

1971, they've played in the national championship game 16 times, winning 11 of them.[27]

Like most collegiate sports programs Syracuse has instituted, there's an expectation that their players will complete off-season training and conditioning. These exercises are important to coaches so they can ensure their team members stay physically fit for the start of their season. They consistently follow-up with their players because a large part of their success in the season hinges on their fitness. All players take part in and push each other to undergo this training. They understand the purpose of the activities they are assigned throughout the off-season.

The Syracuse lacrosse team has an off-season workout specifically aimed at building endurance, meaning the athlete can recover quickly after pushing their body to their fastest speed. Hal Luther, the director of strength and condition for Syracuse lacrosse, regularly administers the 440 Test at the beginning of pre-season camp to identify which students exercised. This is a form of follow up. Members of the team are not able to practice until they have passed the test.[28]

The 440 Test consists of four sprints in which players run the length of the field back and forth. Since the field is 110 yards in length, the number of yards for each test equals 440 yards, hence the name. Players must complete three reps of the sprints within certain time limits with a short break between the passes. The first rep must be completed in 63 seconds or under; the second rep in 68 seconds or under; and the third rep in 72 seconds or under.[29]

This hard work has proved not just useful but necessary to the success of the program. In the 2009 NCAA championship game, Syracuse versus Cornell, the former fell behind early in the game and tried with little success to break through Cornell's defense. Their opponent controlled the tempo of the game and looked to be on their way to their first national championship in over 30 years.

As the game dwindled down to its final moments, it became clear that the Syracuse players could push themselves harder than their opponents. They beat the Cornell players down the field and finally found ways to get through their initially impenetrable defense. Coach Luther observed this when Syracuse midfielder Matt Abbott ran off the field for a few minutes, completely exhausted; to his surprise, Matt claimed he was "nearly 100 percent and ready to go again" and rushed back out.[29]

Their diligence during the offseason paid off for the Syracuse players when they needed it the most. They scored two goals in the final three minutes of the game, including one with four seconds left, to send the game into overtime. It was at that point Syracuse rode their momentum to victory, the eleventh national championship in the school's history.

When those in an organization understand and believe the work that their leader assigns is meaningful, they'll be motivated to put forth 100%. This abstinence from "busy work" leads to trust between individuals, and effective follow up relies on that bond. Without that trust, people won't care about the work they do, and leaders will not be invested to see it through.

The Joys of Busywork

When I was stationed at Wright-Patterson AFB in Dayton, Ohio, I was assigned to help develop the logistics framework for a new Air Force weapons system. I'd just come into the office as they finished putting together documents that detailed the program's foundation. At that point, the government was waiting to see which of the bidding companies would win the contract over the production and management of the weapons system.

Entering the program at that stage meant there wasn't much work to do until a contract was awarded. My supervisor, trying to keep me busy, delegated occasional tasks. I originally attacked these duties with eagerness, wanting to be a productive member. As time went on however, I realized from a lack of follow up that these activities were not for my development or the program; they were just a way to keep me occupied. This epiphany killed my motivation.

I was eventually loaned out to the F-16 program office, which contained meaningful work for me. To be entrusted with this type of task and regularly asked about it was a welcomed change after months of feeling useless. Immediately, I felt rejuvenated and more focused when I began my workday. The labor I accomplished during my time at that office shaped my knowledge of Air Force logistics in a way that would've been impossible had I been continuously tasked with busy work.

People appreciate feeling useful in their positions and desire work that inspires them to do more – and it's even better when their boss discusses their progress with them. The assignment of meaningful work motivates both the leader and those in the organization to communicate on a regular basis about how things are going. Busy work is a surefire way to paint tasks as a waste of time to all parties involved.

Attention to Detail

One of the hardest skills as a leader is to stay organized and pay close attention to detail; this is because they're often required to manage numerous moving pieces within their organizations simultaneously. Still, anyone in a position of power should know what work is being done and by whom, so they can follow up effectively. A leader must hold themselves accountable for overseeing all of their organization's actions.

That Guy's a Machine

An exemplary leader with a remarkable eye for detail can be found in the character of Terry Benedict from 2001's *Ocean's 11*. In the movie, a career conman named Danny Ocean assembles a team of criminals to rob three Las Vegas casinos, all of which are owned by Terry. Even though he's portrayed as the antagonist, Terry is a meticulous businessman who knows everything that occurs in his establishments. He follows up on all oddities to make sure his people are performing to his standards and his customers are having the best experience possible.

In the planning stages of the robbery, Rusty – Danny's right-hand man – sends a member of the team, Linus, to tail Terry for a couple of days to identify a weakness the team could exploit to pull off their $100 million-dollar heist.

Rusty: Okay, tell me about Benedict.

Linus: That guy's a machine. He arrives at the Bellagio every day at 2 P.M., same car, same driver. He remembers every valet's name on the way in. Not bad for a guy worth three-quarters of a billion dollars. Offices are upstairs. He works hard, hits the lobby floor at 7:00 on the nose. He spends three minutes on the floor with his casino manager.

Rusty: What do they talk about?

Linus: All business. Benedict likes to know what's going on in his casinos. Likes to be in control. There's rarely an incident he doesn't know about or handle personally. Then [he] spends a few minutes glad-handling the high rollers… He's out by 7:30 when an assistant hands him a black portfolio. The contents: the day's take and new security codes. Then he heads to the restaurant. Like I said, a machine.

Rusty: And that portfolio contains the codes to all the caged doors?

Linus: Uh huh and, two minutes after they have been changed, he has them in his hand.[30]

During this scene, Rusty and Linus realize how difficult it will be to rob a man like Terry, not just because of the security he has installed, but because of how involved he is in his organization. He has unprecedented knowledge of the workings of his organization down to the smallest detail of knowing the names of his valets. As Terry says to different people during the movie, he "sees everything that goes on in [his] casino."[30]

Most leaders may not have the same level of attention to detail as Terry to follow up effectively (almost obsessively), but they need to be aware of what's going on in their organization. The action of checking in with and actively listening to team members allows leaders to have a stronger impact as well as understand the challenges and successes experienced daily.

Winging It

While serving as Assistant OIC, I had an experience that showed me the importance of maintaining the proper attention to detail. One Wednesday morning, I sat with Capt. Leroy at a maintenance group production meeting. It was common for lieutenants to accompany their OICs both to learn how to represent an organization and to offer help. The was reason for my attendance that morning was a little more specific.

Capt. Leroy cared a lot about his men and the aircraft, yet he often struggled remembering the details of the maintenance the AMU performed, especially when briefing leadership. Before the meeting, he had returned from leave, so he did not have the first half of the week to familiarize himself with the progress of the jobs that we were currently working on. I became especially worried when he arrived late, causing his pre-production update to be rushed and unfocused.

The meeting started off normal, but my anxiety grew as Capt. Leroy started making little mistakes. While these errors were minor, I knew group commander Col. Avery did not have much patience for such missteps from his officers. I felt hesitant as the junior officer in the AMU to speak up with the correct answers unless called upon by Capt. Leroy, for I didn't want to undermine him.

Capt. Leroy continued to unravel as he incoherently attempted to answer questions about our AMU's maintenance decisions and our reasonings. Col. Avery doubled down on his explanations, sensing that something was not right. It didn't take long for the colonel to realize that Capt. Leroy did not know what was happening in his organization. It came to a head when the captain's response to Col. Avery's final question was, "Well, I wasn't here the past couple of days, so I don't know what's happening."

That set Col. Avery off; he quickly replied that if Capt. Leroy did not know what was going on, he had no business representing his AMU in that meeting. Less than two weeks after that confrontation, our AMU received a new OIC, and Capt. Leroy was reassigned to a position in the squadron that didn't require as much attention to detail.

Capt. Leroy wasn't a bad officer, but his lack of focus and attention to detail prevented him from obtaining the necessary follow up to be successful. For a leader to thrive in any field, they must be vigilant when it comes down to what's happening in their unit. Only then will their follow-through and spread of information be effective.

Be Invested

Effective follow up requires a leader to be invested and to participate in their organization's operations. Those in charge have the unique opportunity to be as involved or as hands off as they see fit; it largely depends on what industry a leader is in as each requires varying degrees of engagement. Regardless of field, everyone in a leadership role needs to be attuned to what happens in their organization.

Ignorance Isn't Always Bliss

In the hit film *Iron Man*, Tony Stark is a billionaire genius who graduated MIT with two master's degrees at the age of 19 and used his expertise in technology to expand his family's company to become a leader in military weapons contracting. From the start, Tony's character is shown as an unbothered leader who isn't concerned about his company as long as he is able to maintain his lavish lifestyle. In fact, he leaves his responsibilities as CEO to his mentor, Obadiah Stane.

On a trip to the Middle East to pitch his company's newest development, Tony is ambushed and kidnapped. He is held by what seems to be a terrorist group and forced to make advanced weapons. He escapes by making the prototype for what would go on to become the Iron Man suit. The realization that terrorists are using Stark products to cause destruction horrifies him.

This insight causes Tony to go through a crisis of conscience as he recognizes his lack of investment in his company's dealings has cost people their lives. Determined to rectify that mistake, Tony announces that Stark Industries will no longer be involved in the weapons business.[31]

Although the consequences for a leader's blatant involvement are often not being abducted or imprisoned by terrorists, the takeaway is that individuals who aren't engaged forfeit the opportunity to shape the direction of their organization. If leaders utilize their chances to effectively follow up, they play an active role in the overall success of their team.

The Weight of Command

Another example would be the story of Capt. Roy Cox who, in the early months of the Korean War, was called to lead his field artillery battery reserve unit into active service. This consisted of men from his hometown of Richfield, UT and the surrounding area.

While in Korea, they faced some of the fiercest and most dangerous combat seen during the war. In one battle, they had to repel a direct assault by hundreds of enemy infantry soldiers, an attack that had recently overrun and destroyed other field artillery batteries.

Another night, the situation became particularly dire when enemy infantry poured through the frontlines into the rear areas occupied by the artillery. The captain wired the field telephone lines into his tent and ordered numerous perimeter guards to phone him personally each hour throughout the night. This kept the guards awake, but it also meant that Capt. Cox had scores of interruptions to his sleep. When questioned after the war on why he would do this, his response was amazing: "I knew that, if we ever got home, I would be meeting the parents of those boys on the streets in our small town, and I didn't want to face any of them if their son didn't make it home because of anything I failed to do as his commander."[32]

Early in the morning after his nearly sleepless night, Capt. Cox led his men in a counterattack. They captured over 800 prisoners and suffered only two wounded. He was decorated for bravery, and his battery received a Presidential Unit Citation for its extraordinary heroism.

Capt. Cox's investment in the safety of the men in his squad resulted in the type of follow up few leaders can match. On his shoulders rested an immense responsibility. In the end, his connection and investment in these individuals were responsible for some of his men making it home alive.

This model goes a long way to show how important it is for a leader to care about their people – "mission first, people always," remember? When a leader remains invested in their organization, effective follow up becomes a natural instead of a forced action.

Ask Effectual Questions

There are many factors that comprise a leader who follows up. One of the most important and applicable skills, however, is how to ask effectual questions. In our youth, many were told that "there's no such thing as a bad question." In the workforce and in leadership roles, this is especially true because a question signifies interest and a desire to learn more, which are emotions we want to encourage. However, there *is* a distinction between effectual and noneffectual questions.

Putting Issues Under the Microscope

Once a month, each AMU was asked to present their Health of the Fleet (HOF) findings before group leadership. At such briefings, a single representative discussed prevalent issues facing the aircraft in their unit and what actions were being taken to prevent these going forward. This required the person tasked with the HOF to comb through all the information from the previous month's aborts, breaks, repair times, and other variables. The difference between a successful and an unsuccessful HOF brief was whether the officer briefing had asked effectual questions when reviewing their organization's metrics.

When I prepared the HOF presentation, I found that preparing data would not only give me a snapshot of where my organization was, but lead me to specific questions about how we achieved those numbers. Through asking effectual questions, I better understood the trend of, for example, rising repair times on simple jobs. Instead of assuming maintainers were being inefficient, I dug into statistics and identified anything that could apply to repair time length. Was it logistics delays? Did more severe maintenance have to be performed on the aircraft?

What I found by going through and examining the data was that there was an influx of inexperienced maintainers performing those tasks as training. This was a process I could – and did – improve now that I knew it existed. When it came to the briefing, it was easy to tell the difference between who had settled for the overview of their unit and who had dug deeper. People who prepared comprehensive documents shined during these monthly meetings.

MISSION FIRST, PEOPLE ALWAYS

A leader must seek more than surface-level information to gain a stronger and more nuanced understanding of the issues within organizations – or else those challenges cannot be handled.

The primary attribute of what makes a question an effectual one is if it assists you in identifying the root cause of a problem. By root cause, I mean the factor (or factors) that, if corrected, would solve whatever issue your organization is facing. One doesn't always have to know immediately how to solve these challenges, but they must be able to determine what factors led to them. Being able to utilize effectual questions in the follow-up process is an invaluable skill for a leader to develop because every detail and statistic matters when it comes to optimizing workflows or strengthening their team.

Like a Fine-Tooth Comb

The 2002 Winter Olympics serve as a case study of how effectual questioning by leadership can completely change the course of an organization. In 1999, the events meant to be held in Salt Lake City looked worrisome. The Olympic Games had been weighed down with allegations of a bribery scandal, and their funding sat well below their basic operational needs. Many around the country involved with the athletic festival had already begun conceding defeat.

It was at this point that the Olympic Committee turned to Mitt Romney, who was fresh off his failed bid for the U.S. Senate, to take the reins: "Romney was cast by Salt Lake leaders as the 'white knight' who would put the Olympics back on track. The scandal had deeply demoralized the local staff and threatened to sour sponsors as the committee sought to raise the final $400 million needed to meet its original $1.45 billion budget."[33]

Romney started right away, questioning the committee on how the money was being raised and where that wealth was going. He scanned the budget line by line, determining where they could save or reallocate funds and examining what was legitimately necessary to make the events happen. Romney's ability to effectually question his organization resulted in big changes in the operations of the Olympic Committee by relocating their

Washington office from a luxurious and well-appointed law firm to a barren third-floor walkup; by removing catered lunches for board meetings (and swapping them with pizza at $1 a slice); and by deferring his own $280,000 annual salary until the Games were over.

Though it was difficult, the course-correction of the Olympic Games under Romney's leadership was historic. Before he was put in charge, the Games were mired in debt and impropriety. He transformed the 2002 Olympic Games into an event that ended up earning a $120 million profit. Utah Governor Gary Herbert said the following of Romney: "He turned what was really a bunch of lemons into a really sweet lemonade and what is now arguably – and I think it's true – the best Olympics in our history."[34]

Asking effectual questions takes more than just a cursory glance at budgets and production numbers to be able to identify underlying issues within an organization. Leaders have to be involved and aware of what's going on with the individuals they employ at all stages of work.

Listen to and Act on Answers

The final and possibly most important step of following up is to listen to your people's ideas and opinions. Often, leaders become so entrenched in the courses of action that they only pay attention to the feedback that falls in line with their personal views. This tendency presents a danger that may result in them overlooking valuable information that could not only improve their production but the team's morale. Supervisors need to hear and discuss their employees' inputs to glean more understanding when undergoing the follow-up procedure and be prepared to act on it. In short, the steps should proceed in the following order: listen, learn, think, and act.

MISSION FIRST, PEOPLE ALWAYS

O-Ring Disaster

On the morning of the January 28, 1986, the Challenger waited to lift off from the Kennedy Space Center in Florida. This was going to be the tenth launch of the Challenger and the twenty-fifth space shuttle launch in U.S. history. However, on that day – 73 seconds into the dispatch – the Challenger exploded, killing all seven of the crew members, including five astronauts, one payload specialist, and one civilian.

NASA and the rest of the world watched in disbelief. The launch had been extremely high-profile due to it being the first time a civilian – a schoolteacher named Christa McAuliffe – would be venturing into space. An investigation concluded that the root cause of the shuttle's failure was the failure of the O-rings at the bottom of the rocket boosters which allowed flames and fuel to leak into the external fuel tank, which exploded instantly.[35]

The ironic part of the tragedy was that NASA leadership had taken all the correct precautions: their employees had checked and double-checked the shuttle before departure. They had done everything right it seemed – until they had received word from five of their rocket-booster engineers that launching that morning was not safe and, thus, they should delay the send-off. The temperature that day was 36 degrees Fahrenheit, at least 15 degrees colder than previous launches. Such low temperatures, the rocket-booster engineers explained, would harden the O-rings and not allow them to properly seal. The engineers understood that this element increased the risk of lift off.[36]

After considering the concerns of the engineers, NASA leadership decided to press forward because it had already been delayed five times. They thought this would be their last chance until spring and that would've been a major blemish for such a high-profile mission. Their decision to not listen to the opinions of their experts led to devastating results.

The responsibility of leadership can be a burden at times. Since major decisions rest on a supervisor's shoulders, they can occasionally feel heavy and burdensome, especially because the results of those decisions always come back to the person who made them. Pressure might cause some to rely solely on their own judgment and ignore dissenting opinions. This cannot happen as a two-part leader. The only way to successfully follow up is by listening to and, when appropriate, acting on the responses.

For the Greater Good

Nelson Mandela was elected the first Black President of South Africa, serving in the office from 1994 to 1999. Only four years before being elected, President Mandela had been serving a 27-year prison sentence for treason against the government for leading the South African Communist Party. He was a Marxist who viewed communism as the only way for his country to become a land of equal opportunity. During his time in prison, he spent hours explaining the evils of capitalism to his guards and fellow prisoners.

Nelson Mandela was a prominent revolutionary figure, seen around the globe as one of the forefront activists for social equality. His election sparked joy to those who felt he would overturn the failures of the previous regimes. But for some, his rise concerned people who believed their businesses and livelihoods would be taken under President Mandela's rule.

When he came into office, he did not implement the hard-left socialist policies that many expected him to; instead, he introduced capitalistic and business-friendly methods. These increased the country's economy at record-breaking rates and helped it gain admittance to the World Trade Organization (WTO) in 1995. How'd this happen? Did President Mandela suddenly transform from a lifelong Marxist and activist to a capitalist in the matter of a couple of years?

He did what few leaders have the strength to do: he put his personal feeling aside and listened to others to determine what would be the best for the South African public. It turns out that, before President Mandela stepped into his presidency, the World Bank had created a unique program targeted toward advancing the country's economic growth. They analyzed studies, policy discussions, and study tours in collaboration with all the political parties.

When given the results of this investigation, President Mandela did not fight them. He chose to act on the recommendations of the World Bank, which united political parties in moving the South African economy forward. This decision eventually doubled the growth of the economy, enabling South Africa's poorest citizens to gain access to basics amenities, like running water.[37]

A crucial part to following up is listening to the answers leaders receive, no matter how much such results or data might clash with their own beliefs. Those in leadership positions owe it to themselves, their teams, and their organization to truly entertain and evaluate outside opinions. Anyone able to do that – even in personal relationships – will gain a new skill and have more productive conversations. They might even change their original thoughts on a subject.

Follow-Up

Follow-Up Reflection Questions

- Do you know what happens in your organization on a daily basis?

Assign Meaningful Work

- What's the work that you routinely assign to others?
- How does that work contribute to the success of your organization?
- If it isn't helpful and the tasks err on the side of "busy-work," think about why you give it out. How could you change that?

Be Invested

- How often do you follow up on assignments you've delegated?
- What are the statuses of all major projects and sections within your organization?

Ask Effectual Questions

- Is your organization consistently experiencing the same internal issues?
- If so, what are the root causes for those problems? After you have the causes, brainstorm some solutions too.

Listen to and Act on Answers

- Consider some recent feedback you've gotten from a team member and write it down.
- How do you organize the results of your follow-up?
- Where does input from those in your organization currently fall into your planning process?

4

TIME MANAGEMENT

The 309th AMU owned 22 aircraft, 15 of which needed to be prepped daily for training missions. With the inevitable system breakdowns and malfunctions that would happen throughout the shift, we often found ourselves short of what we needed for the following day.

It was the responsibility of the maintainers who worked the swing shift (2 p.m. to 12 a.m.) to troubleshoot and repair the aircraft for the next day's flying schedule. If the workload proved too great one night and the maintainers were unable to prepare enough aircraft, the pilots would either fly without a spare or cancel some of their flights. This frequently started what is known as the "maintenance death spiral," which is a situation where the AMU would continue using (and breaking) aircraft after aircraft until those that demanded upkeep piled up. The AMU couldn't keep up with the repairs as units deteriorated and, without something to stop the spiral, operations would halt completely. One solution to end this was weekend duty where we brought in a crew and worked while no flying was taking place. This prepared us with all the aircraft we needed for the coming week.

About six months after I was assigned to the 309th, we received a new assistant superintendent, Senior Master Sergeant (SMSgt) Nemo. He reviewed our operations for several weeks before he challenged how we managed the repairs of our aircraft. He did not criticize the effort or speed at which our maintainers did their jobs; rather, he focused on how we decided which aircraft to work on. SMSgt Nemo's contention was that, by aiming our efforts on the aircraft with the shortest times of repair, we could avoid the "maintenance death spiral" entirely. His aim was for the AMU to course-correct without having to ever work weekend duty again.

We followed the SMSgt Nemo's advice and changed the way we prioritized the aircraft – working according to the time of the maintenance job instead of the order they arrived – and our mission capable rate for the aircraft rose dramatically. Utilizing our efforts more effectively impacted not just the missions but the morale of the maintainers. They didn't constantly feel rushed, overwhelmed, or under pressure, which allowed them to perform their best.

Time is the one commodity that equally constrains every industry, just as it constrains us as human beings. Leaders make many choices throughout the day which dictate the direction of their organization. These include decisions of how they spend their own time and what they have their people spend time on. It's up to those who wish to be two-part leaders to make sure that the way time is spent in their organization serves to maximize their potential for success.

Be Intentional with How You Spend Your Time

Those within an organization watch their leaders to see what's important to them, and when the leader puts special emphasis on something, it becomes well-known to everyone in the organization. This creates a great opportunity to steer the focus of their organization without having to make any official statement.

No Detail Too Small

In the movie *Jobs*, Ashton Kutcher portrays the real-life events of Steve Jobs as he creates the technology titan known as Apple. In one scene, the protagonist's team finds itself on a tight deadline to complete development on the Macintosh computer system. Despite the immense pressure they are under, Jobs maintains that certain aspects of the computer that, while not necessary for functionality, are vital to the user experience. He pays attention to the fine details, allowing their device to showcase a plethora of different styles and fonts.

Today, having the choice of different fonts seems normal, but when Jobs created the Macintosh, such a project was seen as extreme, unnecessary, and time-consuming. In the film, Jobs emphasizes the importance of developing typography and pressing his team to make it a priority. When a lead engineer tells the Apple founder there is more important work that needs to be done during their time-crunch, Jobs fires him on the spot.[38]

Jobs doesn't want the Macintosh to be just another computer; he wants it to be a new and unique experience for the user. This message is made loud and clear to his team when Jobs not only fires his lead engineer, but dedicates time to developing seemingly minor aspects.

Leaders influence the actions and priorities of those within their organizations by how they spend their time. If a leader uses their workday for anything self-serving, that can become cancerous and erode the trust of the team. But if they focus on activities meant to sustain the interests of the unit, that shifts the entire cohort's attention to toward those same tasks.

Walk the Line

When performing upkeep on aircraft, precision and safety are two of the most significant elements. This is something we would preach every day to the maintainers, who held an enormous responsibility as any overlooked mistake could have serious implications to the aircraft or the pilot's life. One of the safety precautions maintainers were required to do was to check their work area for foreign objects (FO) after they finished working on an aircraft. The FO was any material or debris left anywhere on the flight line; these objects could be anything from a pen someone dropped to a loose pebble. Why did the airmen do this? Fighter jets have powerful intakes and, when the engines start, they suck up anything in front of them, causing damage to the intake blades or the engines themselves. This was referred to as foreign object damage (FOD); it meant something as small as a loose bolt could take down a multimillion-dollar unit if unnoticed.

To avoid FOD, every shift began with a debris check (also known as a FOD walk) no matter how much work waited for us. Everyone – including the airmen, supervisors, flight chiefs, and others in leadership – in the AMU spread out along the length of the flight line and scoured the entire area. I walked the line beside my people to show the maintainers more than any lecture ever could how important it was to leadership to keep the flight line safe.

Leaders can send out memos, reminders, and have as many meetings as they want, but a team is more likely to notice actions. Those in leadership positions must proactively choose what message they're sending with how they spend their time and be sure to manage their people accordingly.

Value Time as a Resource, Yours as Well as Others

My father had many pearls of wisdom he shared with me to help me become a responsible adult as I grew up. One of his favorite adages was: "If you're five minutes early, then you're on time; if you're on time, then you're late." Many in the military also believe this. There have been multiple instances I have witnessed in which people were barred from entering a meeting because they arrived after the commanding officer.

Valuing time is not only important for those within the organization but for the leader as well. Being punctual tells those around you how much you value them and the work they produce. In my first assignment, I had a squadron commander, Maj. Passan, who was consistently late to meetings and events with his fellow officers. Although he was personable and loved talking to his people, his bad habit ended up negatively defining his leadership style by causing his meetings to run over and keeping others waiting. Maj. Passan developed a reputation throughout the squadron of being unreliable.

In one instance, an airmen received a special award from the major command, and Maj. Passan wanted to be the one to present it to him, so we planned the ceremony around the major's schedule. The AMU lined up in formation five minutes before the appointed time, had the airman's family seated, and a photographer poised to capture the event. The OIC and I waited outside ready to greet Maj. Passan and call the room to attention. Ten minutes passed and the major still had not arrived. At the 30-minute mark, Maj. Passan pulled up and rushed from his car. When he came into the room, he apologized for his tardiness before he presented the award. While everything turned out all right with the actual event, the major damaged his relationship with the AMU, the airman, and his family by keeping them waiting.

"In a Gentle Way, You Can Shake the World"

Leaders must acknowledge their punctuality influences others' perceptions. One leader who understood the value of time and importance of keeping to a strict schedule was Mahatma Gandhi, who gave up all material possessions to live a life of simplicity and service. A relatively unknown fact about the nonviolent revolutionary was that he kept a watch. He was aware of and infuriated by the stereotype of Indians always being late; if they were ever to progress, they needed to learn the value of their time. For this reason, Gandhi famously had no tolerance for tardiness from anyone, including himself. Even during his term in prison, Gandhi dedicated his hours to service his followers and improving himself. "During his stints in jail as a prisoner of the Raj, Gandhi would often write more than fifty letters [to his followers] a day – even when his thumb and elbow ached – in addition to spinning, reading the *Gita* or works by John Ruskin, learning Urdu, cooking, and cultivating his passion for astronomy."[39]

Leadership in itself is a responsibility that comes with the expectation that the person accepting this role will use their time appropriately. They should show up on time, be prepared, and support their organization in any way necessary. People who do not understand this concept risk losing the respect of their team and letting important duties slip through the cracks.

Prioritize What Deserves Your Attention

There are many demands and time-constraints placed on a leader's daily agenda; this comes with the territory as the primary decision maker for an organization. If leaders do not prioritize their time based on the importance of tasks, they will quickly become bogged down with unessential duties.

Good, Better, Best

Dallin H. Oaks, a general authority in the Church of Jesus Christ of Latter-day Saints, explains that cost in a sermon entitled "Good, Better, Best." He preaches:

> We should begin by recognizing the reality that just because something is good is not a sufficient reason for doing it. The number of good things we can do far exceeds the time available to accomplish them. Some things are better than good, and these are the things that should command priority attention in our lives.
> A childhood experience introduced me to the idea that some choices are good, but others are better. I lived for two years on a farm. We rarely went to town. Our Christmas shopping was done in the Sears, Roebuck catalog... For the rural families of that day, catalog pages were like the shopping mall or the Internet of our time. Something about some displays of merchandise in the catalog fixed itself in my mind. There were three degrees of quality: good, better, and best. For example, some men's shoes were labeled good ($1.84), some better ($2.98), and some best ($3.45).

> As we consider various choices, we should remember that it is not enough that something is good. Other choices are better, and still others are best. Even though a particular choice is more costly, its far greater value may make it the best choice of all.[40]

Elder Oaks illustrates how people can spend their time doing good things, but still find themselves falling behind because they are not focusing on the best – or most important – task. The implementation of this concept relies on a leader being able to identify which tasks are vital to their organizations. Developing this judgment skill enables leaders to effectively manage their time.

The Eisenhower Matrix

General Dwight Eisenhower was the commander of the American military during WW2 and was named the first Supreme Allied Commander of the newly created North Atlantic Treaty Organization (NATO).[41] In these roles, General Eisenhower was well-known for meticulous planning and strategizing. This organizational prowess led him to victories in Operation Torch and on D-Day.

General Eisenhower extended his leadership beyond the military, parlaying his success into the political arena by winning the presidency in 1952. There, he accomplished many milestones, such as establishing the National Aeronautics and Space Administration (NASA); adding two states, Alaska and Hawaii, to the Union; creating the Department of Education and the Department of Health; and signing legislation that funded the interstate highway system.

In 1954, President Eisenhower spoke to the World Council of Churches about the underlying principle for his success, which would later be called the Eisenhower Matrix. He said, "I have two kinds of problems: the urgent and the important. What is important is seldom urgent and what is urgent is seldom important."[42]

Time Management

The Eisenhower Matrix[43] was built from this basic idea and has since aided leaders in time management. The purpose is, much like Eisenhower stated, to determine the two types of issues: the urgent and the important. Every task will fall under one, both, or neither of those categories. Once a leader classifies which category each assignment falls into, they overcome the natural tendency

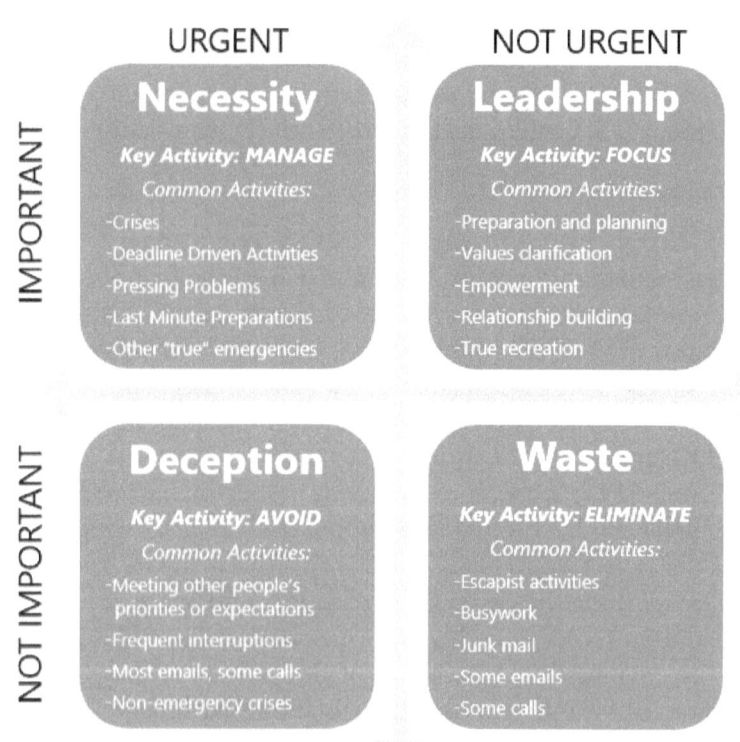

to spend their time on low-priority items.

Time is one of a leader's most valuable resources. If they do not discriminate between what does and does not deserve their immediate attention, they won't effectively lead their organization. It is necessary for all new leaders to develop and hone this skill of time management to prevent wasting resources and energy.

MISSION FIRST, PEOPLE ALWAYS

Make Time to Talk to Your People

Getting to know and connect with colleagues is vital for any leader to do to keep a pulse on their organization. Those carrying out duties at different levels – such as those who see the frontlines of the operations – have unique perspectives and can provide valuable insight to the positive and negative impacts of their everyday decisions. Despite the obvious benefits of making time for their people, like a more enjoyable workplace environment, there are opportunities for leaders to learn more about what is going on beneath the surface.

"Impossible Things Are Happening Every Day."

In 2013, Douglas Carter Beane reimagined the 1957 Rodgers and Hammerstein musical *Cinderella* and brought it back to Broadway. In this version, the audience meets Prince Topher, who is experiencing an identity crisis. The show opens with the prince vanquishing a fierce monster as his royal entourage sings his praises. While fighting this creature, he croons about how he feels unfulfilled and questions his purpose; he believes a ruler should use his time for more meaningful activities.

Prince Topher stumbles upon Cinderella and falls in love with her beauty and kindness for those around her. As they get to know each other, the prince learns about the poverty his citizens face which shocks him, for his advisors had hidden this issue. He is deeply affected by the revelation that the plight of his citizens was being overlooked.

The prince now understands what he can accomplish with his title. At Cinderella's request, Prince Topher meets with other peasants and commonfolk who suggest changes to the kingdom. Prince Topher agrees and creates a new arm of government: an elected Prime Minister to represent the people.[44] This new position provides his subjects more say in what laws are made.

Making the time for those in their organization builds a foundation for a leader to uncover issues that they would have no way of knowing otherwise. Without digging into issues at the ground level, a leader is unable to assist in change.

Time Management

Airmen Breakfast

The Aircraft Maintenance squadron commander I served under, Maj. Passan, instituted bimonthly meetings called Airmen Breakfast which required the attendance of several members of each AMU's leadership to join him for breakfast as a way to glean information from the ground level. What were they worried about? What did they find difficult in their work? How could their leadership better support them?

I was lucky enough to be able to attend the breakfast with one of my airmen and observe Maj. Passan's interactions with others from the department. What I took away was how little the major talked compared to the airmen. When he did speak, it was to clarify a comment already made or to connect with them on a deeper level.

A leader's schedule is something that, if not strictly managed, fills up until it overflows with requests and meetings from every possible avenue for which they are responsible. If they aren't on top of their planning, they can go extended periods being uncommunicative with one of their main stakeholders: their own people. It's a conscientious effort to block out time to connect, to listen, and to build trust. Leaders who make this happen will find they're able to guide and support their team better.

Take Time to Plan, Think, and Develop

Although unfortunate, not all of a leader's time can be spent at breakfast or in team-building activities. Occasionally, the best way for them to improve is to think, plan, and work on their personal development. It serves no one if the head of an organization is constantly on the go; leaders who choose that route are likely to burn themselves out or make a mistake.

MISSION FIRST, PEOPLE ALWAYS

Time Out

Warren Buffett is the CEO of Berkshire Hathaway, an American multinational conglomerate holding company, and one of the one of the most successful investors in U.S. history. A millionaire by 32, Mr. Buffett was an early supporter and investor of some the most successful companies of his time: Costco, Walmart, Coca-Cola, American Express, and Apple. He is known to many as the "Oracle of Omaha" for his ability to predict the direction of the economy. For this reason, he's seen as a "thought leader" ranging on topics from tax reform to the role of emerging technologies.[45]

One might expect Mr. Buffett's days to be chaotic and occupied with meetings because of his industry. While that undoubtedly fills part of his schedule, he understands the importance of processing his day alone, which is why he blocks out periods to do just that. Mr. Buffett has said, "I insist on a lot of time being spent, almost every day, to just sit and think. That is very uncommon in American business... So, I do more reading and thinking, and make less impulsive decisions than most people in business." He further elaborates on this point, explaining, "What's needed is a sound intellectual framework for making decisions and the ability to keep emotions from corroding that framework."[46]

It's obvious Mr. Buffett understands that decision-making is one of the most important responsibilities and skills a leader can have. Whether this means taking time to read, exercise, or receive extra training, this downtime prepares those in leadership roles to meet their tasks with a renewed vigor.

The OODA Loop

John Boyd serves as another example of taking time out of his workday to think. He started his military career as a fighter pilot in the Korean War, though, by the end, he was considered one of the greatest strategists of his time. At 33, Boyd wrote *Aerial Attack Study*, which outlined the best tactics for dogfighting – but his most significant contribution to modern military strategy is the OODA Loop, a decision-making process that revolutionized the

Time Management

way that the U.S. military approached conflict. Its acronym can be broken down into the following: observe, orient, decide, act.

Because of its success, the OODA Loop was adopted by leaders in business, sports, and government.[47]

Boyd's method is particularly useful for making decisions in circumstances that are continually evolving. Before any action is taken, a person must observe all variables at play and then orient themselves by figuring out how this information sways their next choice. They decide, act, and watch how everything unfolds.

The OODA Loop consistently emphasizes the importance of leadership, reviewing all available information and contemplating about the repercussions before acting. It allows a leader to take the necessary time to formulate and execute on ever-changing conditions one faces in any organization. As the OODA Loop illustrates, with each decision comes a new set of variables.[48] If a leader is not taking everything into account, they will most

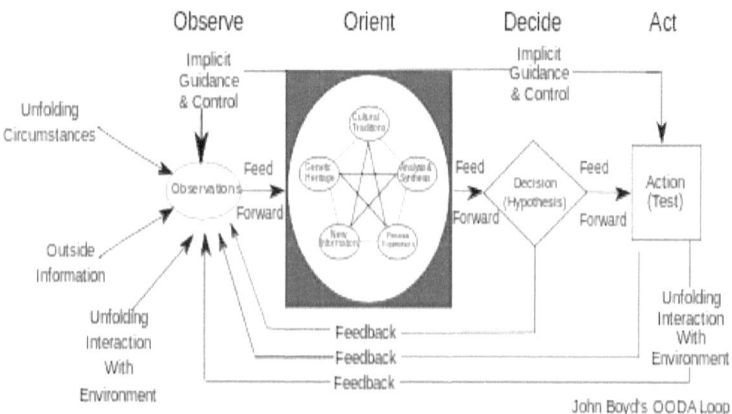

John Boyd's OODA Loop

likely miss something important.

People are naturally impatient creatures, which can make it difficult for both leaders and their people to not have immediate action on every issue within the organization. What they (leaders more so) need to understand is that sometimes, inaction is not wasted time. When people take the time to plan, think, and develop ideas before jumping into a situation, they provide the best chance for their own growth and long-term success.

Use the Force!

The Jedi are mystic monk-like knights who travel the galaxy to restore peace and establish justice wherever needed within the *Star Wars* franchise. This specialized group uses the energy of the universe around them – famously deemed as "the force" – to complete their missions. Such power allows wielders supernatural skills like telekinesis, control over weak-minded individuals, and the ability to sense suffering of others.

In *The Phantom Menace*, Jedi Qui Gon Jin and Obi Wan Kenobi are sent to protect the queen of Naboo from the Trade Federation, who is planning her capture and the takeover of her planet. While on this mission, Qui Gon finds a young boy named Anakin, whose sensitivity to the force is unprecedented. The elder Jedi takes the child with a promise to his mother that he would be trained as a Jedi. Qui Gon brings Anakin before the Jedi Council, a group of highly-skilled individuals chosen for their power, wisdom, or instincts, to obtain permission to train the boy as a Jedi Knight. Regardless of the committee's intrigue by the child's raw power, they want to mediate and ponder on the matter.

The Jedi Council understands the value of taking the time to evaluate and make decisions. As leaders, they have to be certain they exercise their power to help those under their protection. Eventually, they agree that Anakin should not to be trained as a Jedi, for they sense a darkness in his future.[49] If the council's ruling had not been defied, the galaxy would've been spared Anakin's transformation into of one of the most villainous antagonists in cinematic history, Darth Vader.

Leaders need to make sure when their time is spent that it is done deliberately. The decisions they make and the tasks they carry out on a daily basis impact everyone in their organization. This means they must occasionally free their minds through rest, focusing on non-work-related issues, meditation, or strategizing solutions. Each person in a leadership position should manage their schedules effectively, which includes blocking out time for them to work independently. They will see improvement in what they can accomplish, both for themselves and their people.

Time Management Reflection Questions

- What do you believe are *your* boss's top priorities? Why?
- What are your top priorities within your organization?
- Do you think your people understand what your top priorities are? Have you communicated them?

Value Time as a Resource, Yours as Well as Others

- How often do you feel rushed or overwhelmed throughout your workday?
- What's your organization's culture on punctuality? What's your opinion on the matter?
- Do you believe being on time makes a person more or less effective at their job?

Prioritize What Deserves Your Attention

- How much of your time at work would you consider effectively used?
- What activity or activities should be eliminated from your schedule?

Make Time to Talk to Your People

- How often do you get out of your office and talk to those on the front lines?
- What repeatable event can you create to help you spend time talking to your people?
- What are the top issues your team faces right now?

Take Time to Plan, Think, and Develop

- What training have you gone through to improve your skills as a leader?

Time Management

- ♠ How do you distance yourself from work when you get home, if at all?
- ♠ What do you do for yourself during the week to make sure that you remain focused and involved?

5

HOW TO ENFORCE STANDARDS

In my first job in the Air Force as a flight commander I supervised 150 airmen – but I had no idea how to instill discipline. Movies show officers shouting orders at the top of their lungs, or depict young, enlisted members being whipped into shape with creative punishments. Neither of those seemed like me. I learned through my first assignment that there's no one right way or style for leaders to enforce standards. Over time, I witnessed 30-year chiefs drill Air Force principles into insubordinate airmen and squadron commanders using nothing other than simple questions to allow airmen to be crushed under the weight of their own answers.

The Air Force line of disciplinary action builds in severity as such: record of individual counseling (RIC), letter of counseling (LOC), letter of admonishment (LOA), letter of reprimand (LOR), Article 15, and then a court martial. Issuing paperwork is an important duty officers have; the document(s) an airman receives can significantly affect their career. Once served disciplinary documentation, airmen are given an opportunity to correct their behavior. Should they continue the same erroneous actions, the paperwork and punishment will increase in severity.

I distinctly remember when I issued my first LOC to an airman in my flight. Even though I had observed commanders issue paperwork to airmen in the past, I felt incredibly nervous. The airman waited outside while I counseled with flight chief

SMSgt. Bergeron over what I planned to say. I wanted to make sure I was going to be fair, not a pushover. After discussing strategies, I called the airman in.

He was not a troublemaker; in fact, he was one of our better workers. Unfortunately, he had made a costly error because he didn't pay attention to what was happening around him. In maintenance, this kind of mistake is unacceptable as it can result in people getting hurt or even killed. I knew if I let this incident slide, I would be unable to enforce the standards that were expected in my flight in the future.

I started out by asking the airman simple questions with potentially difficult answers: Do you know why you are standing in front of me today? Explain to me what exactly you did wrong. What are the possibilities that could have resulted from your actions?

If you were in my position, what would you do with an airman that made this mistake? This last question left my airman silent.

When he finally spoke, I watched him realize the potential consequences his actions could've caused to his colleagues and to his career. It was then that I issued the LOC. I explained to him how we still trusted and expected him to perform, but that both our flight and the Air Force had expectations that needed to be met.

Enforcing standards is a responsibility every leader inherently owns, as painful as they may occasionally be. Those in an organization look to their leaders to set the tone of how, when, and with whom those principles will be imposed. Two-part leaders will recognize this burden as an opportunity to shape their organization and people. They will enforce standards in a way to not just discourage poor practices, but to encourage efficiency and effectiveness in the organization.

MISSION FIRST, PEOPLE ALWAYS

Recognize the Importance of Standards

Leaders must maintain order and discipline, which are manifested through the enforcement of standards. When a person in leadership chooses not to take this responsibility seriously and allows the rules within their department to slip, chaos quickly fills the void. This degrades their reputation as well as the efficiency and productivity of their people.

"This Lamb Is So Undercooked, It's Following Mary to School!"

My wife and I love Gordon Ramsay; we've been to his restaurant in Vegas and are fans of his TV shows. Chef Ramsey is an amazing chef, but his culinary skills aren't what has made him a cultural icon. He is a man whose fame is based on the rigid standards he has for himself and the chefs around him and the refusal to fall short in any aspect.

In Ramsey's *Kitchen Nightmares*, which can be found in both the U.S. and the U.K., Chef Ramsey visits a failing restaurant and observes how the establishment handles service. A few of the common issues the renowned chef pinpoints are toxic work environments, personal challenges among the staff, and inefficient basic operations. The problems Chef Ramsey uncovers all have the same root: the owners of the restaurant do not recognize the importance of the basic standards required for operating a functional restaurant and, therefore, do not enforce any kind of rules.

For example, there is always a surprising amount of filth when Chef Ramsey inspects the walk-in freezer, which is where food is stored before preparation, of a given restaurant. It's supposed to be organized, well-stocked, and, above all, sanitary. Yet he discovers trash, rotting food, improperly stored ingredients, and sometimes even rodents. In this sense, the restaurant owners do not administer proper expectations or standards.

Chef Ramsey make suggestions on how to save the crumbling business, though they rarely have to do with creating new culinary masterpieces. His solutions are more focused on owners integrating standards within their restaurants. Regardless of these changes seeming simple, more often than not, the owners struggle to implement Chef Ramsey's principles. These cannot be a one-time change but a consistent effort from leadership. Those who put in the energy to uphold these expectations thrive in their new chapter.

    A leader who follows through with the standards they've imposed within their organization signals to the world and to their employees that there is a commitment to quality. We see this in Chef Ramsey's shows as well as his multiple restaurants and bars. Given time, these expectations become more than a benchmark; they flourish into a company culture that recognizes and strives within beyond basic guidelines or codes.

"Some Day My Prince Will Come…"

    Another example of this is Disney, a company whose name synonymous with quality. Whether it's animation, amusement parks, or Broadway musicals, Disney delivers superior products for people of all ages to enjoy. It could even be said that this corporation aims to surpass all of its previous successes. This has made them an integral cornerstone of family entertainment in homes across the world. The culture of enforcing high-quality standards started with the company's namesake, Walt Disney.

    He set the standard for what he expected to be the quality of a Disney product to be with his first full-length animated film, *Snow White and the Seven Dwarfs*. Leading up to the film's completion, Walt and his fledgling company were becoming more known in the entertainment industry for the innovation and imagination of their animated shorts. At an early stage in his corporation's career, Walt knew to set himself apart. It was not enough to rely on past successes; he had to push toward a bigger goal while maintaining the same level of excellence.

    While making *Snow White*, Walt engaged with multiple aspects of the production process to ensure the final product would meet the Disney Company standard. This included overseeing the story generation, animation management, and implementing new ways to improve the impact on their wide range of audiences. He pushed his employees to create special and memorable scenes, discarding much of their early work, which might've passed as acceptable at other studios. He wanted the standard for a Disney film to be more than mere entertainment – it should emotionally connect with viewers. Because of this, he insisted his team develop characters in a way that audiences would be frightened at their danger, weep at their failures, and rejoice in their eventual triumph.[50]

The urgency for such a high-caliber work led *Snow White and the Seven Dwarfs* to tremendous critical success. In 1938, it took the country by storm, winning multiple awards and bringing in more box-office revenue than any animation in U.S. history.[51] *Snow White* marked one of the earliest stages for Walt Disney to expand his creative vision, producing countless classics. In each of the company's subsequent works, Walt and all those who would later hold his position continued his culture of quality, manufacturing through the implementation of the standards that he set.[52]

Leaders who understand the importance of standards and enforce them, encourage a diligent output of work that's of value. Expectations provide the foundation for any organization's culture, which will attract and retain employees who are able to meet or exceed them. The maintenance of specific values and production standards allow leaders to grow their organizations while not losing sight of what has made them successful.

Increase Standards to Increase Performance

However, it's not enough to maintain the performance of their organization; a leader should always search for ways to improve overall performance. Raising the standards pushes everyone to see what they're capable of and to inspire innovation. Should a manager fail to incite this change or pressure, their skills and their employees' progression can decline due to complacency, slowly chipping away at their combined efficiency.

How to Enforce Standards

Continuous Improvement Process

In the early 1980s, Motorola was plagued by substandard expectations, and they were losing business because of it. They struggled to contend with the competition from emerging and innovative Japanese companies. To find a way to gain an advantage over their rivals, Motorola's CEO Bob Galvin made a commitment to provide better employee training and raise the standard companywide to improve their production.

Mr. Galvin launched a program in 1986 developed by two veteran engineers at the company known as "The Six Sigma Quality Program." This policy set a benchmark of what amount of deviation (or error) was acceptable in production.

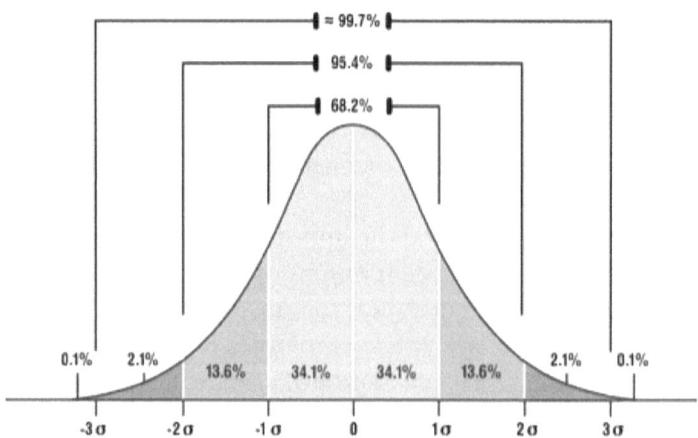

Operating an organization at a one sigma level meant that, for each one million units of production, there will be 691,000 units with variability or – in layman's terms – 69% of them will be defected. An increased level of sigma symbolizes the decrease in irregularity, and the gold standard was marked at six-sigma of quality production. This meant that, for each one million units created, there will be 3.4 errors or .00034% of defected items.[53]

This is an ambitious program. In fact, it is difficult for an organization to receive a six-sigma certification.[54]

MISSION FIRST, PEOPLE ALWAYS

The certification requires the implementation and enforcement of a company's processes down to the lowest level of activity to ensure there's no room for error. If at any point during the procedure, there is waste or inefficiency, the entire workflow must be revamped.

Companies like General Electric, Honeywell, and Bank of America that have achieved this six-sigma status are considered pillars in their industry.[55] Their success can be directly traced back to their pursuance of and committing to standards for excellence. These organizations exemplify how to triumph and maintain it from the imposition of quality-related rules.

All effective leaders hold a common aspiration regardless of what industry they work in because they want to see how successful their organization can become. Implementing and constantly reviewing standards are ways for those in leadership roles to push themselves and their people to see what they are capable of. When these guidelines are balanced with the welfare of their staff, leaders and the businesses they work for can rise to greater heights than previously imagined.

Miracle on Ice

In the early 1900s, the U.S. had a history of consistently having one of the top three hockey teams in the world each year. However, later in the twenty-first century, the country found itself consistently never rising above fifth place in any international tournament because the Soviet Union had become the new dominating force. As of the 1980s, the U.S.S.R. had won the last four Olympic gold medals, going 24-1-1.

Herb Brooks was fresh off winning his third NCAA championship when he took a position as the new U.S. Olympic hockey coach for the upcoming events in Lake Placid. He wasted no time; after choosing his players, he instilled a new system of play, focusing on competing at a faster pace and relying on creativity to take advantage of opportunities to win. Due to this quickened pace, Coach Brooks held his team to a higher standard of conditioning than ever before. He also created a more competitive schedule leading up to the Olympics. He felt that, by testing his players more than they had been previously or than any other squad, they would be better prepared to face any opponent in the world.

George McPhee, one of Herb Brooks' players, commented on his coaching: "Herb's real ability... was being able to push people beyond where they thought they could go... He was not a fun guy to play for, but you had to respect his understanding of the game and what he was trying to accomplish."[56]

The higher standards that were set for this team paid off; it was at these Olympic Games where the U.S. hockey team won its first gold medal in decades. Their training led to them being able to consistently out-skate other teams late in the matches. While opposing players grew tired, Coach Brooks' athletes continued making plays down the stretch. In the semifinals, the U.S. team beat the U.S.S.R. This match became known as one of the greatest upsets in the history of team sports and is now known as the "Miracle on Ice."[56]

When a leader sets high standards for their team to achieve, increased and maybe even surprising results will follow. The key to this is knowing how far you're able to push your people. One of Coach Brooks' strengths was his understanding of his players' limitations and encouraging them to surpass challenges they had previously thought were accomplishable.

Furthermore, establishing principles will ultimately reduce waste and increase the output of an organization – though it requires an active leader who must take a pragmatic look at how they're currently operating and note where to improve.

Create a Culture through Enforcing Standards

Whether they realize it or not, when a leader chooses which standards to administer, they're instilling more than rules and procedures. They're creating a culture for their people as they project values and priorities for them to follow.

Leave It to the Chief

When my father, a retired navy commander (CDR), took over the Naval Reserve Unit at Minneapolis-Saint Paul Joint Air Reserve Station, he was welcomed with a tour by his chief. As a reserve officer, my father – referred to as CDR Johnston – was not embedded within the unit; he'd only visit once a month after traveling from Idaho. He understood the challenges and the dangers that came with commanding remotely, and he wanted to make sure everything was in order to do the job correctly. CDR Johnston had to ensure the sailors met the standards, even without him physically being present. Upon inspection, CDR Johnston found the unit fully functional, but there was something that bothered him. At the end of the tour, he pulled his chief aside and said, "Chief, I've noticed many of the sailors have their hair longer than regulations allow. Is this something I'm going to have to deal with?"

The chief promptly replied, "No sir, you leave that to me." CDR Johnston arrived the following day and found all of the sailors had new, shorter haircuts and freshly pressed uniforms.

CDR Johnston admitted to me that he knew cutting their hair wouldn't necessarily improve their tasks, but he wanted to set the tone that he followed regulations and held everyone to these high standards in his organization.

A culture of enforcing standards cannot appear without involvement from leadership. They have to not only maintain the standards themselves, but explicitly push others to. Once those in an organization see their leader cares about the policies and guidelines, that mentality trickles down to every level.

Semper Fi

The U.S. Marines is one of the first examples that come to mind whenever people think of a strong enforcement of rules. This branch prides themselves more than any other on discipline; they wear it like a badge of honor. For Marines, the act of meeting guidelines is part of their identity and shapes how their organization runs. Their positions aren't simply a job for them, but a way of life that many hold onto long after they retire from active service.

I witnessed firsthand this commitment to their high standards when I oversaw my airmen on a short tour for training at the Miramar Marine Air Base. My unit tried to retrieve our room keys after a long day of driving, but no one was at the desk to help us obtain them. After a couple of minutes, a small Marine corporal – who looked no older than 18 – appeared, apologized for the wait, and checked us in. I didn't think twice about it until about 20 minutes later when I walked by the front desk again and noticed that same corporal yelling at a much larger and more intimidating private for leaving the area vacant. I realized that day that, for the Marines, it didn't matter whether you were on the front line or working the front desk, you are expected to meet their high standards.

While not all organizations expect their people to achieve Marines-level standards, creating a culture of discipline perpetuates success for any organization. These rules could include simple aspects like dress codes and policy on break times, and they could also cover weightier matters like behavioral or performance expectations. As leaders learn to correctly leverage these standards, they show to build compliant team members and establish a solid organizational culture.

My Pleasure!

While on a road trip with my wife, we wanted to eat somewhere we knew would provide a good experience. There is one place we both agree on: Chick-fil-A. Since opening its first standalone location in 1986, the restaurant has become one of the most successful fast-food chains in the world. While they cook tasty chicken, statistics show another reason for their success – their standard of service.

MISSION FIRST, PEOPLE ALWAYS

In 2020, Chick-fil-A claimed the Number One spot on American Customer Satisfaction Index's annual restaurant report for the sixth year in a row.[57] This is not an accident as Chick-fil-A works hard to build and foster a culture of service. On their website, they mention their standards in a single sentence: "We may be in the restaurant business, but really, we're all about serving people." Obviously, their mission manifests itself through their employees' actions.

Before opening a Chick-fil-A location, potential franchisees are put through a rigorous interview process in which only 0.4% are accepted to guarantee the standard that customers have come to expect from Chick-fil-A. Once they're accepted, Chick-fil-A has very specific requirements for each establishment.[58] These expectations go down to the smallest details like tables having fresh flowers, and every staff member responding with "my pleasure" when thanked. Khalilah Cooper, Chick-fil-A's director of service and hospitality, addresses the reason the company has such strict standards for each franchise: "We have this really... generous approach to our guests and we want them to feel restored and cared for – not necessarily that it's like home for them, but it feels warm and inviting and that they want to come back..."[58]

It is the adherence to these standards that has created the level of customer service that Chick-fil-A strives to maintain. Leaders make decisions every day that will contribute to the culture of their team; what standards are set and enforced determine the stakeholders' experiences. For this reason, a leader needs to know what culture they want to build before they choose which principles and values to instill.

Use Standards to Create a Safe Environment for Your People

People thrive in safe workplaces, therefore it's a leader's primary responsibility to protect that atmosphere. The standards organizations choose to abide by are in place not only for the quality of their work, but for the wellbeing of their people. When rules are relaxed or ignored, dangerous situations can arise.

How to Enforce Standards

Chernobyl, 1986

The Chernobyl Nuclear Power Plant in Pripyat, Ukraine conducted a routine shutdown one day in 1986. It was part of a test to determine how long the turbines would supply power to the main circulating pumps following a loss of the main source of electricity. Preempting this examination, the undertrained operators disabled the automatic shutdown mechanisms which left the nuclear reactor extremely unstable. When the control rods were inserted, a dramatic power surge ensued which formulated steam. This pressure proved too great to be contained, forcing the reactor to explode, releasing fission products into the atmosphere.[59]

Two of the plant operators died in the initial explosion and destruction of Chernobyl. One hundred and ninety-two tons of radioactive fuel discharged in the environment, killing 28 others through radiation poisoning. Within a month of the reactor explosion, 116,000 people who lived within a 30-kilometer radius had to be evacuated and relocated because of the widespread contamination.[60] Chernobyl is remembered as the greatest nuclear disaster in the world.

As we know now, nuclear energy is a perfectly safe energy source when operators take the proper cautionary measures. A leader owes it to their organization to enforce the standards that keep people safe, even in less extreme industries like customer service. With guidelines disregarded or unspoken, it can create an environment where individuals continually push to see what they can get away with; thus, those in leadership will lose control of their staff's behavior. This might be relatively harmless for most organizations; for instance, maybe people come into work late or take long breaks. For other fields, the consequences can be far more severe.

The Uniform Code of Military Justice (UCMJ) is the guiding document of statues for military behavior while on and off duty. Section 92 states unprofessional relationships are prohibited, including any relationship between officers and enlisted members as well as any relationship between those of different ranks within the same chain of command. One of the reasons for this is to maintain the power balance that exists within a hierarchal system. This is true in many organizations, though even more so in the military where, if an individual of higher rank gives someone else a command, they are expected to obey completely.

Betrayal of Trust

In 2011, a young female trainee at Lackland AFB accused her male drill instructor of sexual assault. This opened an investigation that found at least 31 women who were victims of sexual misconduct by their drill instructors at the same location. This misbehavior ranged from secret consensual relationships to rape and using influence to gain sexual favors. Anu Bhagwati, a former Marine Corps officer, illustrated the troubling situation these women were in a 2012 CNN article:

> You cannot do anything without requesting permission from your drill instructor. You cannot use the bathroom, you cannot move from left to right, you are literally in many cases a robot waiting for permission to take a step. And if you have that relationship, which is based on fear and intimidation... if that's the person you're asking help from, it becomes a very bizarre scenario.[61]

In November of that same year, the Air Force completed its investigation which consisted of over 280 investigators and support personnel. This team attributed the breakdown in standard of training to three elements: weakness and gaps in institutional safeguards, insufficient leadership oversight, and inadequate self-policing by instructors. General Edward Rice, commander of the Air Education Training Command at the time, said the Air Force would be implementing 45 recommendations based on these three elements over the next year.[62]

While these three factors were key in allowing this toxic culture to take root, at the core of each of these was a disregard of standards. Negligence like this does not manifest all at once; it happens little by little. Maybe a leader noticed an instructor flirting with one of his students but chalked it off as innocent. These inappropriate actions snowballed until it was considered typical, and more people felt they could get away with such.

The policies and rules of any organization are tied to leadership's willingness to either let them be disregarded or to reinforce them with vigor. Leaders must understand that, by enforcing standards, they maintain the efficiency of their organization equally as much as they protect their staff.

Do Not Allow Exceptions from Standards

For a leader to successfully guide an organization, they cannot show favoritism to any one group or person. The application of varied standards creates an imbalance, like a "death spiral." Obviously skewed preferences breed resentment and potential conflict. To keep any organization unified, leadership must make sure their policies apply to all without marginalizing or restricting anyone.

The Honor Code

Brigham Young University (BYU) is a private university in Provo, Utah that's owned by the Church of Jesus Christ of Latter-day Saints. All students who attend must sign an honor code in which they sign a set of standards that go above and beyond most universities' rules. Some of the guidelines are as follows: to abstain from alcohol, drugs, pre-martial sexual relations; and to remain well-groomed. These rules may seem extreme – especially for those in their early to mid-twenties – but the students who attend this school understand and agree to adhere to these standards.

In the 2010-2011 basketball season, BYU's team had been in the middle of a fairytale season. They were in possession of the eventual player of the year, Jimmer Fredette, who scored 28.9 points per game and was poised to make a run in the NCAA tournament. BYU had just beat their rival, San Diego State, and climbed to the number-three team in the country, a feat that had never been achieved in the university's 136-year history. But then news broke that Brandon Davies – the team's starting center – had been suspended for the rest of the season based on honor code violations.[63]

The suspension spurred discussion on sports TV and radio programs across the U.S. Pundits argued back and forth on whether this measure was warranted for actions that, at another university, would not matter at all. BYU faced enormous pressure externally and some internally to reconsider Davies' removal. Those who opposed the suspension could not understand why the university was seemingly throwing away their first chance at a national championship for their self-imposed code of conduct.

BYU, however, stood by its decision regarding Davies and ended up losing in the sweet sixteen of the NCAA tournament. Even though it cost them the opportunity to possibly play for a national title, the university chose to stand by its standards as a religious establishment. Selective implementation of discipline is one of the quickest ways to lose credibility. Those in leadership cannot be choosy when it comes to who in their organization has to maintain standards.

A leader in any industry must realize their decisions will come under scrutiny from others, both inside and outside of their organization. If they want to be able to maintain credibility, they have to remain objective and fair, looking past any biases. They need to be clear with everyone what the ground rules are and what is required to achieve success.

Harvard's Diversity Problem

Asian-Americans are consistently one of the most successful minority groups across academics, professional milestones, and financial achievements. As of 2015, Asian-Americans filled up many rosters in America's top universities. While only representing 5% of the population, they represented

How to Enforce Standards

22% of Harvard's freshmen class and 26% of MIT's.[64] Despite this impressive feat, Students for Fair Admissions filed a suit against Harvard University in 2014, claiming the institution unconstitutionally discriminated against applicants of their ethnicity by requiring them to test higher than any other race to be admitted. Statistics agreed with Students for Fair Admissions: Asian-Americans were being held to a higher standard than Whites, Blacks, or Hispanics. The data from the admission board showed an Asian-American student scoring 1460 on their SAT (32 on the ACT) was valued the same as a White student scoring 1320 on the SAT (28.6 on ACT), a Hispanic student scoring 1190 on the SAT (28.3 on the ACT), and a Black student scoring 1010 on the SAT (24.5 on the ACT).

Such inconsistent standards resulted in a loss in confidence in the leadership at these universities. It's difficult for those in an organization to see expectations applied differently for the same actions because it causes issues, whether it's intentional bias or not.[65] Those who find themselves being unfairly treated by unequal enforcement of rules will lose faith in any of the decisions that come from leadership.

Allow Yourself Flexibility in Enforcement

This may seem at first glance a direct contradiction to the last section. How can a leader not allow exceptions in the enforcement of standards but still be flexible? The difference is in outlook versus application. Part of being a leader is evaluating all of the variables in a situation and making a decision that will positively affect the direction of an organization. It is the responsibility of the leader to use measured judgment and consider everything before acting.

As a newly-promoted 1st lieutenant, I was mentored by senior enlisted members, one of whom was SMSgt. Norman. When leadership decisions needed to be made, we would close the office door and weigh the options. We'd discuss everything from whether we needed to bring people in on weekends to how to improve the unit's morale. A common subject we chatted about was how to discipline those who had not lived up to the Air Force standards.

Leadership in the military has a lot of discretion when it comes to disciplining those in their unit. I realized upon speaking with SMSgt. Norman that I wanted to standardize our disciplinary actions: every time a person does X, they will receive Y. He immediately taught me how to be a situational leader. Each event that leads to some form of punishment cannot be treated the same because not every person is the same, not all motivations are the same, and not all violations are the same. In order to succeed, we must look at all the factors of a specific situation and select the option that helps the individual in the long run.

Letter of the Law

The NCAA has been known as an organization that diligently enforces rules. In the spring of 2018, this tendency reared its head once again when the organization ruled that C.J. Harris – a high school senior who had been offered a preferred walk-on spot on Auburn's football team – was ineligible. He was uncompliant with the NCAA's marijuana policy due to the cannabis oil he has been prescribed to help him deal with his epilepsy. After previously suffering 14 seizures, C.J. had found that the use of this oil eliminated his seizures completely. Despite his medical condition, the NCAA treated C.J. the same as a player who recreationally smoked pot in their car.[66]

When leaders are unable or unwilling to differentiate and insist on treating every situation the same, they lose the trust of their people and even outsiders. Being a situational leader is more difficult than just ruling by the letter of the law. It takes actual thought when you approach cases of discipline instead of trying to shove square pegs through round holes.

Allowing Creativity in Discipline

Lt. Col. Holland, a commander I served under, further expanded upon my education of what it meant to be situational

How to Enforce Standards

leader. Normally, when disciplinary actions reach his level, the airman in question has done something quite serious; the guilty party has already gone through their supervisor, the section chief, *and* the flight commander. At this point, the airman is usually looking at being court-martialed and discharged.

Every time an airman came before Lt. Col. Holland for disciplinary action, the lieutenant-colonel would go through the same process. He would have the offending airmen and those who passed him up the chain of command visit his office and ask the offending airmen if they knew why they were there and to explain what had happened from their perspective. Though he might've asked a question or two during the description to clarify for understanding, he mostly listened.

After hearing out the airman, Lt. Col. Holland would excuse the individual and go in order from the front-line supervisor to the flight commander, requesting each person's recommendation for disciplinary action and why. He wouldn't move onto the next person until he was satisfied with the answers from each leader. Lt. Col. Holland did this in part to teach everyone how to think critically through situations, but to make sure he had all the information he needed to make a fair decision.

If he felt that the airman wasn't ever going to be able to conform to the Air Force's standards, he would discharge them. If Lt. Col. Holland felt they could grow but needed to adjust their attitudes and/or behaviors, there were different options: the traditional route of docking the airman's pay or issuing them mounds of paperwork; or the assignment of additional duties, like cleaning detail for ten hours of scrubbing. There were even instances that 5,000-word essays would be assigned to the airman to help him understand why accountability was vital for a 20-year-old airman.

These creative and insightful decisions Lt. Col. Holland arrived at often left me impressed. Not because there was anything inherently genius about the punishments themselves, but because he took the time and energy to consider what action could help the individual airman instead of taking the easy path.

The most successful leaders are those who understand what their people need and act on that instinct. Paying careful consideration to each situation can be difficult since it requires extra effort for a leader, but it is necessary. As leaders put forth the effort to treat their people as individuals – which may call for distinctive methods of enforcing standards – they can expect to get more productivity and satisfaction out of them.

How to Enforce Standards

How to Enforce Standards Reflection Questions

- What standards or rules are in place in your organization?
- Do people's compliance to those standards affect everyday operations? How?

Increase Standards to Increase Performance

- Are the standards for the work achieved in your organization the highest quality that your people can achieve? Why or why not?
- Do you know what the potential of your organization is?
- How could you find out?

Create a Culture Through Enforcing Standards

- How would you describe the culture of your organization?
- Are the standards of your team a reflection of that culture?

Use Standards to Create a Safe Environment for Your People

- What massive misconduct (professional or personal) could take place in your organization that would violate the rules and standards in place?
- If there aren't any you can think of, brainstorm what guidelines are already upheld to avoid these problems.
- How would enforcing current standards prevent an organization-wide misconduct?

Do Not Allow for Exceptions to Standards

- What standards do not apply to everyone?
- Why are there differences? Is it intentional bias or discrimination?
- If you don't hold everyone equally accountable within your organization, what message are you sending those to whom the standards apply?

MISSION FIRST, PEOPLE ALWAYS

Allow Yourself Flexibility in Enforcement

- ♣ Is it possible for two people to commit the same infraction but have varying degrees of culpability?
- ♣ How can it be helpful to tailor the consequences for infractions to the individual situation and person?

PEOPLE ALWAYS

Motivating your people to perform at their highest levels

6

VISION

Col. Kuchard entered as the commander of my ROTC unit during my third year in the program. He envisioned teaching us cadets more fully about one of the Air Force's core values: excellence in all we do. Before Col. Kuchard's arrival, Detachment 855 was a ROTC unit that performed well in everything we did from our unit's average GPA to drill team performances. However, his mission was to raise the bar even higher; his main target for this improvement was the physical training (PT) program.

The purpose of the PT program was to foster teamwork and leadership opportunities, instill discipline within the unit, and prepare all cadets for the Physical Fitness Assessment (PFA). Every ROTC detachment participant is required to take the same PFA as an active-duty Air Force member each semester to stay in good standing with the program. The PFA was divided into four sections at the time – waist measurement, 1.5-mile run, sit-ups, and push-ups – with points awarded for how each of these are carried out. For both ROTC and the Air Force, the test has a range of cumulative scores from 0-100, in which 75 is considered a passing score. However, cadets who desire to become officers are expected to exceed a passing score. Our average as a detachment was around 92 for the PT test, an above-average score when compared to other Detachments around the country.

When Col. Kuchard shared his initial vision for the Detachment with us, we were stunned to discover that his end goal for PT was to have an average PFA score of 98. This grade was achieved regularly by the fittest cadets, but seemed like a lofty goal for the majority of the members. An achievement of a 98 average on the PFA would make our detachment the highest scoring in the U.S.

Our detachment's morning workouts immediately increased in intensity and effectiveness. This was difficult for many cadets, who had struggled to pass the PFA previously. Each workout pushed everyone to their limit; no matter of their previous fitness level, every cadet found themselves improving each workout. As we gathered at the end of our conditioning, we were reminded of the ultimate goal: a 98 average.

Over the next few semesters, we continued to raise our individual scores to make Col. Kuchard's vision a reality. Pushing ourselves toward that goal motivated us when it felt like we had enough. Eventually, those of us in detachment achieved the sought-after average. What seemed impossible a short time before became an accomplishment through leadership with a distinct vision.

Those stepping into new roles – especially ones in leadership – cannot afford to simply maintain the status quo; they must look to the future and guide their organization toward success. A two-part leader will create a vision of what their people can accomplish if they push beyond their current boundaries. Such a clear objective allows others to buy into it and develop a willingness to move forward despite adversity.

Create a Clear Path to Your Vision

Establishing a vision is vital to motivate and unify an organization. Share your ideas as a leader and inspire your team with a plan to achieve it. Then, as each individual goes through their workday, choices can be viewed through the prism of "How does this contribute to our organizational goal?"

Fork in the Road

Lewis Carroll's classic novel *Alice in Wonderland* demonstrates how Alice follows a white rabbit to a fantasy world called Wonderland. There, she faces peculiar and dangerous adventures that teach her important lessons. One of her first encounters is with the Cheshire Cat, a magical creature who can appear and disappear at will. Upon arriving at a fork in the road, Alice notices the Cheshire Cat lounging in a nearby tree.

Alice: Would you tell me, please, which way I ought to go from here?

Cheshire Cat: That depends a good deal on where you want to get to.

Alice: I don't much care where —

Cheshire Cat: Then, it doesn't matter.[67]

The principle the Cheshire Cat addresses applies just as much to organizations as it does to individuals: when there's no vision of what the future should be, there's no sense of direction. Without a cohesive operational vision, multiple independent agendas manifest to pull people in different directions. Leaders who detail a big-picture overview provide stability and purpose for their team members.

Marvel vs. DC

The Marvel Cinematic Universe (MCU) is a Disney franchise based off the superheroes of Marvel's comic books. These characters, including Spiderman, Captain America, the Incredible Hulk, Iron Man, and Thor have starred in movies and TV shows dating as far back as the 1940s. While some of these characters were already household names, most of them were not known outside of committed comic book fans. The MCU, under Kevin Feige's leadership, began designing a vision like nothing attempted by another film franchise before: to connect independent stories and characters in an all-encompassing narrative.

Vision

The vision of the MCU officially began with *Iron Man* in 2008, with an additional scene after the credits hinting at a larger movie universe. In this after-credits scene, Nick Fury – the head of a secret organization called S.H.I.E.L.D. – approaches Tony Stark in an attempt to recruit him to the Avengers Initiative. The project, eventually shortened to the Avengers, is a team of superheroes created to protect Earth from extraordinary threats. Each movie in the MCU continued to have its own independent story while including pieces of the overall Avengers plot that built what would be known as Marvel's "Infinity Saga." This vision culminated in the 2019 film *Avengers: Endgame*, where the MCU showed the final battle of over 40 combined heroes and villains.

Mr. Feige's vision is realized in each of these movies. Despite the countless directors and actors who worked on each of these movies, Mr. Feige's vision remained at the heart of everything they did; they understood the ultimate concept and assembled their stories accordingly. Under Mr. Feige's guidance, the MCU became the most profitable movie franchise of all time. Five of the ten highest grossing movies of all time are part of the MCU as current data shows.[68]

This unity in vision and direction stands in stark contrast to other movie franchises, like the DC Extended Universe (DCEU) with the iconic characters of Batman, Superman, and Wonder Woman, that have attempted to replicate the MCU's success. While Warner Brothers had plenty of great material to work with, they didn't have a leader with a distinct vision to unite their universe.

The DCEU launched its franchise with its most iconic superhero, Superman, in the 2013 movie *Man of Steel*, which seemed like promising competition for the MCU. The DCEU moved quickly while they had momentum to create other movies within the universe, such as *Batman vs Superman*, *Wonder Woman*, *Suicide Squad*, and *Justice League* – all of which had varying degrees of success. Some of the most dramatic differences were the tone, pacing, and purposes of each movie, confusing audiences who searched for a common thread. These results left the DCEU unsure what path its franchise would take – or if it could even continue.

The vision a leader shares with their organization can unify individuals and enable them to make informed decisions in the future. It tells team members where to focus their efforts. As those in charge express their thoughts and overarching schemes, they will find their stakeholders working more cohesively. People enjoy their jobs more and respond to being part of a greater mission that extends beyond their own personal sphere.

Safe and Reliable

Three weeks into my new career as an Air Force officer, I attended a change of command ceremony for the Maintenance Group Commander, Col. Anderson. Initially, I didn't understand what this event meant for me. I soon recognized how the group commander was the ultimate authority for everything concerning maintenance on the base; he was responsible for all of the maintenance personnel at Luke AFB and for briefing the base commander on the status of every maintenance operation. At this event, Col. Anderson shared a few words introducing himself and his vision for the maintenance group, which boiled down to this: safe and reliable aircraft.

Col. Anderson's vision for the maintenance group was to emphasize – no matter what other pressures influenced maintainers during the workday – safety and reliability of the aircraft. He wanted this vision to be the lens through which decisions at every level within the group were made. We held a daily production meeting where we briefed him on the status of our aircraft and what we were doing to maintain them. This discussion was our singular guaranteed interaction with leadership; it was the chance for Col. Anderson to counsel young officers on maintenance practices as well as how to formulate better decisions. He always made the point to end the meeting with the same words: "Safe and reliable aircraft."

Vision

This became helpful to me as a new leader who was trying to find his way. When difficult maintenance choices popped up, the first thing I did was refer to the group commander's vision. That simplified all other decisions. Col. Anderson's vision encouraged me to make smart judgment calls at a time when I did not have much experience to lean on; it helped me to form a process how to make decisions with an end goal in mind.

As leaders learn to effectively communicate their vision down to the lowest levels of their organization, they can motivate their people to work as one entity going forward. It gives them a measuring stick with which to compare all their own decisions and goals. With this reference point, all team members better understand how their actions play a part in the grand scheme.

A Vision Is More Than a Plan

A vision is more than just a goal; it's a concept that rests at the core of an organization's overall mission to provide deeper meaning into why people do what they do. People want a set of values or a meaningful roadmap to follow. Many in the workforce today apply to companies that have missions that match their own because it's encouraging to collaborate with like-minded individuals.

"First to the Key, First to the Egg!"

In the 2018 science fiction movie *Ready Player One*, a brilliant programmer named James Halliday creates an interactive virtual world called the OASIS (Ontologically Anthropocentric Sensory Immersive Simulation) wherein people can live out their fantasies. Halliday's vision for the OASIS is to give people the ability to explore countless experiences and to become whatever they want to be. Ultimately, this becomes a source of refuge for millions living in an apocalyptic, crumbling society. One of these players is Wade Watts, who idolizes Halliday and believes in his vision of the OASIS.

MISSION FIRST, PEOPLE ALWAYS

When Halliday dies, he creates a contest within the OASIS in which the winner will be awarded control over the program. Halliday leaves clues in the virtual world that only those who have studied his life and shared his vision would understand. As one of his most ardent followers, Wade adeptly deciphers the hints, outpacing all other competitors.

As Wade grows closer to victory, a corporation named IOI (Innovative Online Industries) seeks control of OASIS. The firm wants to monetize the program with advertisements, upgrades, and other ways that would make them and their shareholders more revenue. Nolan Sorrento, the CEO of IOI, approaches Wade with an offer: if he helps IOI win the contest, he will reward Wade with riches beyond his imagination and an executive position. It is an attractive offer for an impoverished kid. Despite all of the incentives, he refuses because he'd rather give up a lifetime of wealth to keep Halliday's vision pure and intact.[69]

As the contest nears its conclusion, all of the competitors fall away, leaving Wade and the IOI. Between the kid and the final challenge stands an entire army of IOI soldiers, so Wade decides to seek the assistance of other players to help him save OASIS. To Sorrento's surprise, hordes of loyal supporters back Wade, not because he or Halliday are inspirational leaders, but because they believe in the vision of the program.

People within organizations want the answer to how they're going to do what needs to be done, but first, they want to know why. What's the bigger picture? As I touched on, individuals are motivated to work harder for a vision they believe in. Leaders who provide details to the "why" will have stronger organizations due to high morale.

Campaigns That Became Movements

The 2008 and 2016 U.S. presidential elections produced winners who, at first glance, couldn't seem more different: Barack Obama and Donald Trump. Both presidential hopefuls faced off in their primaries and general elections against candidates who were far more qualified than them on paper. But it was the candidates' ability to create a vision that ultimately drew the two elections and candidates together. They inspired and motivated constituents who felt disenfranchised by the bickering stagnation of government and mobilized them to turn their campaigns into movements.

For Barack Obama – the young, charismatic senator born in Hawaii – the word that defined his 2008 campaign was *change* – change to end the partisan fighting and make a "Purple America,"[70] change by electing the first African-American president, change the perception of America in countries throughout the world. Those who voted for President Obama in 2008 felt like they were part of a vision that was greater than themselves; they were a part of history.

In 2016, Donald Trump shocked the world by surpassing a primary field of 16 extremely qualified Republican presidential candidates. He fought his way through them and the general election with the rallying cry that became a phenomenon: "Make America Great Again" (MAGA). This phrase reached those who felt they had been economically and culturally left behind, people who felt the previous administration hadn't believed their problems mattered. MAGA evoked a vision of national greatness, and a country proud of its place in the world.

These leaders understood that, by sharing their vision with their public, they would become more than just a campaign built on policies and political stances. People want to follow a purpose, something more than just working day after day for monetary gain. When a leader demonstrates what their piece of the puzzle is, they take pride in pushing their collaborative vision forward.

Your Vision Should Seize Future Opportunities

Be aware that visions don't always translate into instant success. The value of a leader's idea is often recognized by the long-term impacts of their decisions rather than immediate results. Those who take the time to craft a vision for their organization's future will help their people seize opportunities that have not yet presented themselves.

Father of the Air Force

Consider General Billy Mitchell, the man known as the "Father of the Air Force" for the role he played in the Air Force becoming its own military branch. During WWI, General Mitchell commanded all American air units in France, but at that time, all aircraft operations in the U.S. military fell under the command of the Army Air Corps. In his capacity, General Mitchell saw firsthand how the integration of air power into the battle plans could provide a major advantage in conflicts. Speaking about the role of aircraft in the military, he said, "In the development of air power, one has to look ahead and not backward and figure out what is going to happen."[71]

General Mitchell's views were not popular in the U.S. military. Leadership saw air power as a capability to be used sparingly; to them, General Mitchell's constant badgering for a separate military branch for airpower was annoying at best and reckless at worst. Tensions reached a tipping point when the Army Air Corps completed a demonstration of an aircraft's capability to sink naval warships. General Mitchell utilized these results to show how this force was equal in importance to that in the Navy and Army. He wrote reports and articles, many of which criticized military leaders for not recognizing airpower as an integral part of military strategy.

In 1925, General Billy Mitchell was court-martialed and found guilty of insubordination, which suspended him of his rank and pay for five years.[72] This didn't stop him from touring the country though, preaching to the public about the benefits of airpower for national security. Mitchell died in 1936, just 11 years before the formation of the U.S. Air Force.[72]

Despite that, he's known as a prominent figure in the creation and culture of the Air Force as it is constituted today. General Mitchell was a leader whose vision was ahead of his time because he understood how his ideas would positively impact the long-term success of his country. Some leaders, like General

Mitchell, conceptualize with the future in mind; they plan for tomorrow while everyone is focused on today. When a leader's vision is realized, it has the potential to shift the paradigm of whatever industry they operate in.

Blockbuster's Downfall

Blockbuster was an entertainment company that carried movies, video games, and music for people to rent. From the late 1980s to the early 2000s, the franchise was a household name throughout the U.S., and it became an unspoken weekend tradition for most families to visit Blockbuster and rent movies in their "new releases" section.

In 1997, Reed Hastings, a Silicon Valley veteran, founded Netflix after being spurred by his frustration with $40 late fees he had accrued for returning a movie to Blockbuster after its scheduled return date.[73] His service entered the market of movie rentals with a new business model concept: subscription-based rentals. Customers would pay a flat monthly rate to select as many movies as they wanted (and return them whenever). The company devised algorithms to give viewers suggestions on movies they might enjoy based on previous selections. Netflix emphasized looking ahead to the future of the industry in an attempt to incorporate technology into their process.

In 2000, Netflix approached Blockbuster with a proposition to buy them out for $50 million, but Blockbuster refused that or any other kind of deal.[73] Instead, they focused money and resources on their inventory and creating a positive in-store experience for customers. They were at the height of their power and viewed Netflix's attempts to modernize the industry as a fad. Unfortunately, their leadership didn't have the vision to see how their disregard for improving their product would be their eventual downfall.

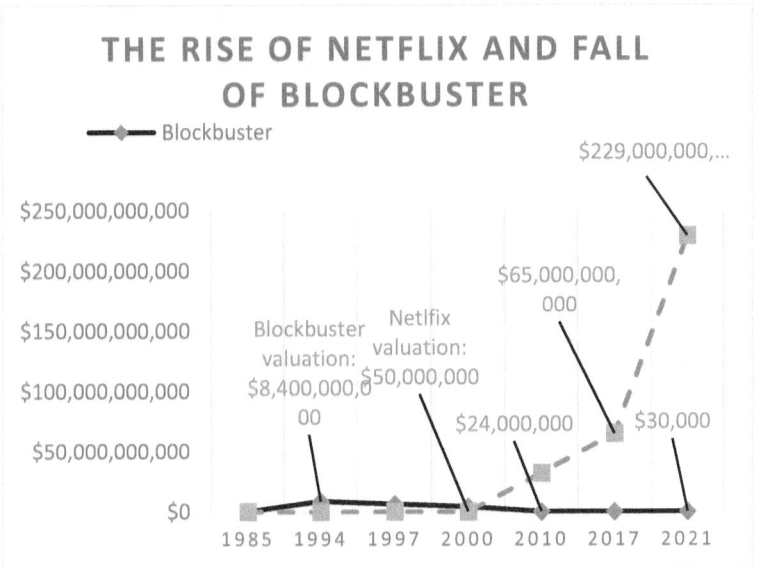

Sloan, Molly. "Netflix vs. Blockbuster – 3 Key Takeaways." Drift. June 1, 2020. https://www.drift.com/blog/netflix-vs-blockbuster/. Values reflect Netflix Enterprise Value, YCharts, July 2021. https://ycharts.com/companies/NFLX/enterprise_value

In 2007, Netflix switched its primary business model from DVD rental subscription to streaming services. With this move, its customer base grew by 20% that year, taking more of the market share. Blockbuster realized too late that, due to its leadership's lack of vision, it was now dealing with an emergency as its customers increasingly depended on a competitor for movie needs. Blockbuster attempted to create its own online platform, but was far behind at that point. The effort faltered and Blockbuster went bankrupt in 2010.[74]

Netflix has gone on to not only revolutionize video rentals, but alter how people view media overall. The company has grown from solely providing movies and TV shows to producing them as well, creating several award-winning movies and series. This has set it up to become the primary source of media entertainment for many around the world. By the end of 2017, they had over 130 million subscribers and were operating in 190 different countries.[75] The leadership at Netflix understands how vision is a key component for staying relevant in a time when circumstances are changing rapidly. Those organizations with plan-oriented, forward-thinking leadership will be able to stay ahead of potential issues instead of panicking as they appear.

Your Vision Should Navigate Future Pitfalls

The benefit of an organization with a defined vision is that the people in charge are more likely to see what future difficulties they might face and plan how to avoid them. When there is no plan to follow, they will become consumed by current issues and be unable to address their future until it's too late.

First Line of Defense

The watchman was an individual in ancient Israel whose duty was to stand on the watchtower that overlooked cities, military outposts, and even large vineyards. He served as a guard, warning the people of approaching danger before it arrived. The imagery of the watchman is referenced throughout the Bible, in both the Old and New Testaments. In Ezekiel 33:6, this character's responsibility to the people is emphasized:

> But if the watchman sees the sword come, and blow not the trumpet, and the people be not warned; if the sword come, and take any person from among them, he is taken away in his iniquity; but his blood will I require at the watchman's hand.

In ancient Israel, if the people were ever attacked without warning, the responsibility for their deaths would fall on the watchman. Leaders must carry ownership as the watchmen for their organizations; they must consider potential threats and make decisions that allow them to navigate the ever-changing landscape of their industries. Staff members do not have the necessary information or perspective to strategize future pitfalls, which is why it is largely up to the leader.

MISSION FIRST, PEOPLE ALWAYS

"And Then We'll Teach Them How to Say Goodbye."

George Washington is one of the founding fathers of the U.S, and his name has been permanently etched into American history as the commander of the Continental Army, the president of the Constitutional Convention, and the first president of the nation.[76] In all of these positions, Washington made decisions that shaped the future of the fledgling country he was establishing.

During his time as a public servant, Washington was the most universally beloved man in the new land. When the time came for America to select its first president, he became the first and unanimously elected leader. In 1792, President Washington repeated the feat, running virtually unopposed. It was under his leadership that the country established important financial, domestic, and international policies that still affect our government today. To ensure the survival of the U.S. as a functioning Democratic Republic, he stepped down at the conclusion of his second term.

He knew, as everyone else in the country did, that he could remain president for the rest of his life if he wanted. President Washington understood, however, that the vision of America was larger than one person – after all, the American people had just fought a war to shed the yoke of monarchs with delusions of divine providence. He wasn't going to let his new country take on another lifelong ruler. By stepping down, he set a precedent and created a blueprint as to how we could have a peaceful transition in leadership. In his farewell address, President Washington sought to warn his people of future issues. In the opening paragraphs of his speech, after announcing his retirement, he issued counsel for the country in preparation for his departure.

> Here, perhaps, I ought to stop. But a solicitude for your welfare, which cannot end but with my life, and the apprehension of danger, natural to that solicitude, urge me, on an occasion like the present, to offer to your solemn contemplation, and to recommend to your frequent review, some sentiments which are the result of much reflection, of no inconsiderable observation, and

which appear to me all-important to the permanency of your felicity as a people. These will be offered to you with the more freedom, as you can only see in them the disinterested warnings of a parting friend, who can possibly have no personal motive to bias his counsel. Nor can I forget, as an encouragement to it, your indulgent reception of my sentiments on a former and not dissimilar occasion."[77]

      President Washington also outlined several traps that would create difficulties for the American people in the future: the reliance on political parties, incurring a large national debt, losing appreciation of religion and mortality, and more. His warnings proved more prophetic than even he could have anticipated. Many of the greatest problems we find ourselves facing in this country today stem directly from our failure to follow President Washington's visionary counsel.
      To guide their people successfully, leaders need to look ahead and address future issues that could impact the continual success of their organizations. As they put this into practice, they will gain the confidence of their people. Understanding how your organization has to adapt to meet these challenges is something you, as leaders, must be able to do in order to succeed. Leaders who have a vision can identify areas of improvement to their industry more readily and make the necessary adjustments. Those who are too blind or scared to make those changes will become obsolete.

Vision Reflection Questions

- ♠ What vision is your organization working toward?
- ♠ Is everyone unified in that vision? If not, how can you motivate those who maybe aren't as attached?
- ♠ Was this vision created and communicated by you?

A Vision is More Than a Plan

- ♠ What about the work you do in your organization motivates you to give your 100%?
- ♠ Do those in your organization feel the same way? Why or why not?

Your Vision Should Seize Future Opportunities

- ♠ What upcoming challenges does your organization face?
- ♠ Are there any opportunities you and your team are looking forward to?
- ♠ How are you preparing now to navigate those future challenges?

Your Vision Should Navigate Future Pitfalls

- ♠ Think back: Did you initially have difficulty getting your staff to buy into your vision? Why or why not?
- ♠ What positive impacts have directly resulted from your organization following the vision that you set forth?

7

TRICKLE-DOWN ATTITUDE

The 309th AMU had the lowest flight production of any group when I first arrived. This was accepted by both wing and group leadership. Not only did the 309th have fewer aircraft than others, but its aircraft were the oldest in the entire fleet. We often flew 14 sorties (flights) a day – eight in the morning and six in the afternoon – but some days, due to aircraft availability, we were only able to produce 10.

Our group commander, Col. Avery, called the entire AMU leadership into his office one day to inform us that the Air Force was experiencing a shortage of fighter pilots. Luke AFB, whose primary mission was to train officers, was heavily impacted by this news. Not only were we dealing with aircraft shortages, but now we had to increase the rate with which we prepared F-16 and F-35 pilots. For our AMU specifically, this meant flying 22 sorties a day instead of 14.

We felt what Col. Avery expected from us went beyond the capability of both our people and our aircraft. It seemed like he was setting us up for failure. He listened to our objections, thought momentarily, and then described the situation further. This was not a request; the Air Force *needed* more pilots and we had to provide them. Although he knew it would be difficult, he counseled us to find our "can-do switch."

He understood how the leadership of the AMU reacted to this information would play a vital role in the way those under our commands would also feel. It was a domino effect. If we came out somberly and reluctantly delivered the message to our airmen, we would've failed before we started. On the other hand, if we came out excited and explained that we had been given a chance to prove everyone wrong about our AMU, *that* attitude would trickle down. Even if we did not hit the target numbers, we would improve morale and push our organization to do its best work.

Our AMU OIC made sure that all of us in the leadership team were onboard with finding our "can-do switch," like Col. Avery had advised. Our airmen seemed excited to take the challenge and try to meet the new expectations that had been placed on them. As we began to ramp up our sortie generation, we found our airmen rising to the occasion. Our leadership team continued to stoke this excitement by communicating those successes every day to the whole AMU.

As an AMU we were able to push ourselves and find new and more efficient ways to maintain our aircraft. Ultimately, we not only made most of the sorties required, but operated at the highest aircraft availability rate (time in which aircrafts in an AMU are ready to fly the mission) that the 309th had achieved in years. There were a lot of factors that went into making this successful transition to the new standards, but it wouldn't have been possible had our team members not believed.

Attitude, culture, feel – whatever it is called, it has a profound impact on the day-to-day life of everyone in an organization. Most times, the attitude of the ground level workers can be traced through supervisors all the way to the highest levels of leadership. Most leaders do not understand the influence they wield in this respect. Two-part leaders must recognize the power of their actions on the attitude of their people and learn how to use it to better an organization.

Understand How Your Attitude Affects Your Organization

Leadership attitude affects an organization profoundly because it encourages staff to follow suit. Both the attitudes and actions of leaders tell everybody not just what's acceptable, but what's preferred. This is a power that many are unaware they

Trickle-Down Attitude

possess. Once realized, leaders can use this principle to lift the morale of and motivate people just by shifting their own thoughts and behaviors.

When the Captain's Not Happy, Nobody's Happy

One AMU stood above the rest while I was at Luke AFB; they won the AMU of the Year award every year. This was due in part to their leadership. Capt. Cooper was a small female captain with a larger-than-life personality; she embraced every opportunity to let anyone around her know that she believed her AMU was the best in the Air Force. Each morning, she walked her flight line, reminding her airmen how lucky they were to be part of their AMU. Her attitude was infectious, and it showed in the pride her crew took in their work.

After Capt. Cooper was transferred to another AMU, I noticed an immediate impact on the AMU she'd left behind. It was mostly the same maintainers and technicians that made up the team, but something had changed. They seemed to become haphazard and mistake-prone, and the morale of the people plummeted. I talked to one of the flight chiefs that was assigned to Capt. Cooper's former AMU and asked him what had happened. The details spilled out of him instantly – the new leadership team always seemed flustered, spending most of its time reprimanding and tearing into supervisors for not having the desired answers. This anger spread all the way down to the airmen. In the end, everyone was trying to find a person to blame rather than solutions to the AMU's problems.

There was certainly more going on than just this change in supervision, but the attitude of the leadership team was obviously detrimental to the group's morale. The culture eroded to such a point that no one cared about fixing the problems; they just wanted to survive until the next day.

MISSION FIRST, PEOPLE ALWAYS

Whether good or bad, the attitude of those in leadership roles permeate throughout an organization. As leaders understand the influence their demeanor has on their surroundings and work, they'll be able to improve how they react to situations and better control the atmosphere. This concept of "a trickle-down attitude," however, must be acknowledged for a change to be made, at which point, the supervisor must decide whether they're willing to take the time to create a positive environment.

The Patriot Way

Under the direction of Bill Belichick, the New England Patriots created one of the most prolific dynasties in the history of the NFL. In his tenure as head coach and as of 2021, the Patriots have nearly a 75% winning percentage and have been Super Bowl Champions six times. This means that the team has won as many or more Super Bowls under Coach Belichick than any other team during their entire franchise history. This kind of success is attributed to Coach Belichick and his staff for instilling what they call "The Patriot Way."[78]

When Coach Belichick came to New England, they were $10 million over the salary cap with little to show for it. The Patriots were a team built on a vision of instant success, meaning their plays and funds centered around a few star players. Coach Belichick wanted to restructure his organization around principles that relied on the team as a whole more than any one player. "The Patriot Way" enabled Coach Belichick to bring in unproductive or unwanted players that were considered lost causes by other teams and transform them into vital cogs.[79] Players like Wes Welker, Legrande Blount, Kyle Van Noy, Chris Hogan, and others had been disregarded by every other NFL team, but fulfilled their potential on the field under Belichick. Often, how they performed in New England was unable to be replicated when they moved elsewhere.

"The Patriot Way" is a mindset that applies to how everyone in the organization goes about their profession. It's comprised of a few key principles:

Trickle-Down Attitude

> Put individuals in positions to succeed
> Do your job
> Flexibility is the key to success
> Ignore the outside noise
> No one person is bigger than the team.

These ideas are not just the team's policies but the culture. Coach Belichick is not charismatic; he doesn't handle the media very well and is definitely not prone to inspirational quotes like others. But he is the living embodiment of the "The Patriot Way" in every public action. Nothing demonstrates this more clearly than the team's 2017 Super Bowl victory against the Atlanta Falcons. Many coaches and players would talk about their great success, but at the celebration parade, Belichick spoke about how his team would go right back to work, capping the interview off with a chant of "No days off."[80]

The Patriots embracement of "The Patriot Way" is not just for on-the-field successes, but for their everyday interactions within their communities. It's unheard for a sports dynasty to not to have a cast of stars who make themselves the center of attention. Even Tom Brady – the future hall of fame quarterback who was the Patriots' team captain for 19 years – displayed this attitude when asked how he felt about people considering him the greatest quarterback in the history of the sport. He said, "I still feel like there's still more to be accomplished: working on my technique, on my fundamentals, all the things with my training. I still feel like I can be better."[81]

The attitude of a leader is the first step in creating an organization's culture. People like Capt. Cooper and Coach Belichick exemplify this in how they've built success within their specific fields. When those in leadership make a conscious choice to adopt a positive attitude, it trickles down because that's one of the best ways to create motivation for their people.

MISSION FIRST, PEOPLE ALWAYS

Recognize the Contributions of Your People

Wanting to be recognized for the good things we do at work or at home is a basic desire. Those within an organization yearn to feel seen by their leadership for the hard work they put in each day, which is why those who acknowledge the accomplishments of their people will motivate them to further excel. Many individuals I know are more likely to work harder if they feel cared about. Leaders who neglect giving credit or recognition that's well-deserved will breed apathy and discontent.

The Creation of a Traitor

For many U.S. history buffs, the name Benedict Arnold is synonymous with the word "traitor." This is because General Arnold betrayed our founding fathers during the American Revolution by switching sides in the middle of the war. What many don't realize, however, is that General Arnold was also one the best field officers of his day. Without him, the American Revolution would not have had its early successes.

In 1776, General Arnold correctly predicted that British general Carleton would sail his force through Lake Champlain.[82] In order to cut him off from New York, General Arnold led a smaller group out to meet Carleton and his men. General Arnold stalled the British military until the battle season was nearly over. General Carleton fled with his soldiers back to Canada for the winter without fighting a single battle against the Continental Army's New York Militia.

In the battles against British general John Burgoyne and his invading forces in 1777, General Arnold proved his value again by serving under General Horatio Gates. During the pivotal Battle of Bemis Heights, General Arnold defied orders by taking his forces and directly attacking the British line, setting the General Burgoyne's men into disarray. Burgoyne surrendered his entire army to General Gates at Saratoga after 10 days.[83] News of this victory in Europe was the final push that France needed to make the decision to enter the war on the side of the Americans.

After all of this, how were the British able to convince General Arnold to betray the country he had fought so hard for?

Trickle-Down Attitude

The answer was simple: General Arnold felt immense discontent due to the lack of recognition he received from both the Continental Army and the Continental Congress. After his heroics at Lake Champlain, five junior officers were promoted over General Arnold. He was slighted after turning the tide of the war at Saratoga when General Gates did not mention General Arnold's contributions to the battle and took all the glory for the victory.[84] This lack of appreciation left General Arnold questioning his already-fragile allegiance to the young country. British officer Major John Andre took advantage of this by convincing General Arnold to become what would end up being the most notorious traitor in U.S. history. Arnold's early biography[85] detailed his conversation with Major Andre, writing:

Andre: But what cares Congress or your services, your wounds, and your losses? [...] Your enemies in Congress do not thank you. I have even been told that in your last fight with Burgoyne, when you so crippled him as to compel his surrender, you fought as a volunteer, and without a command; and that while you were leading the troops, Gates was in his tent, not even going upon the field at all; yet he received Burgoyne's sword, a medal from Congress, all the honors of victory, and he, forsooth, is the hero of Saratoga.

Arnold: Yes. All this and more is true; and this, in part, has driven me to my present conduct…[86]

With the actions they choose to display, Leadership affects those working under them. By not expressing recognition for his accomplishments, the Continental Congress helped push General Arnold to the British. When it's clear a leader values their people and their contributions with verbal commendations, they will not only gain their loyalty but receive their best work. General Arnold is undoubtedly responsible for his own actions, but in a different world where the leaders of the American Revolution gave him proper recognition, he might've ended up being one of the country's greatest heroes instead of a notorious traitor.

Victory Friday

While stationed at Wright-Patterson AFB, I worked in the F-16 program office on the radar modification program for about six years. Fifteen minutes before the end of my Friday shifts, all staff received an email to visit the office our program manager, Col. Grigg. Despite being ready to enjoy our weekend, we dutifully staggered to the appointed meeting place, where Col. Griggs asked each attendee to share their biggest achievement from that week, personal or professional. This tradition was known as "Victory Friday." As its namesake implies, it encouraged everyone the opportunity to discuss their triumphs and be recognized by their colleagues.

Once the last individual had shared their win, Col. Griggs awarded who he thought had the biggest achievement as the weekly champion. The trophy of a spartan warrior raising a flag above his head became a coveted prize in the office.

As our leader, Col. Griggs wanted everyone in the program to be acknowledged for the work they did. He understood that our duties weren't always exciting, but he also knew that if leadership showed appreciation for even our small victories, it would motivate us to perform our best. It worked. Personally, I felt more earnest and responsive to his assignments than I might've been otherwise.

When leaders highlight and praise the efforts of their people, it becomes mutually beneficial to each party because everyone feels seen and appreciated to strive beyond basic duties. Leaders who explore their organizations and observe how their people contribute to the overall success gain a greater understanding of their inner workings. They will also form a greater connection with those they oversee. The stronger the dynamic between a team, the more seamlessly operations flow.

Trickle-Down Attitude

Get Out from Behind Your Desk

I learned this lesson while serving as an Assistant OIC in the 309th AMU. While having a discussion with SMSgt. Nemen, an enlisted leader, about how to motivate our people, I asked him, "We've worked together for a while. What have you seen that I can do to be a better leader here?"

He pondered and then told me I had to get out – become a visible leader among the airmen. SMSgt. Nemen counseled me to attend the morning roll calls for each section and announce a positive accomplishment or trend that we as leadership had noticed from them. Roll call is the time at the beginning of the shift when flight chiefs and supervisors make sure everyone is present, assign individuals to aircraft, and give AMU announcements. SMSgt Newmen explained that the more the airmen knew that I appreciated them and their effort, the more effectively I'd be able to lead.

It was a little uncomfortable for me the first time I went to a roll call. I entered right after one flight chief had taken roll, which confused the airmen who weren't used to seeing AMU leadership in these meetings. Before they parted, I asked if I could take a couple of minutes to tell the airmen about how, as a leadership team, we had noticed the extra effort their flight had taken in preventing ground aborts. As I finished, I recognized all of the airmen standing tall and beaming with pride.

I swung by other roll calls and praised different tasks for each section. This ignited and solidified the connection I had with the airmen; I noticed them showing more enthusiasm and putting in extra effort on the flight line. They wanted to continue to prove me right, to demonstrate to me and the rest of leadership that they were an asset.

Leaders who recognize the importance of their people's contributions and take time to commend them will gain both the appreciation and the trust of their organizations. It's important for them to display that authentic recognition of achievements because it motivates their staff to perform at a higher level.

Inspire Your Organization to Push Through Challenges

One of the ways leaders are most often judged by society is if they are able to inspire. Many perceive the main responsibility of a leader is to prepare their organization to meet upcoming challenges. This can be done a variety of ways, but no matter what a leader says or does to create enthusiasm, they have to believe in it too. An individual who doesn't trust in their cause or their people cannot convince anyone to follow them. Corinthians 14:8 drives home this point: "For if a trumpet gives an uncertain sound, who shall prepare himself to the battle?" A leader needs to be passionate about their cause themselves if they ever hope to inspire their people.

Visions of Nature

The TV show *Parks and Recreation* (2009-2015) depicts the parks department of the local (and fictional) government of Pawnee, Indiana. The series details the day-to-day challenges of maintaining land and organizing community activities on a government budget all while trying to build a governing entity by the people, for the people. In the political satire sitcom, the characters attempt to balance the bureaucracy of their office work with doing good in their struggling town.

The parks and recreation department is led by Ron Swanson, a gruff libertarian survivalist who thinks that government is fundamentally useless; he does not believe his office is necessary or even beneficial. Being that he isn't inspired by his own role in the government or the work it does, he hardly stimulates excitement in his colleagues to perform their best work.

Like many parks departments across the nation, a major responsibility of the office is to host activities for its community. In the mockumentary series, one such event is an art exhibit entitled "Visions of Nature," which encourages local artists to submit their work to be presented in a public gallery. As the head of the department, Ron is responsible for giving the opening remarks for the event. His words encapsulate the attitude he holds for his organization and its work:

> Okay, everyone, shut up! Welcome to Visions of Nature. This room has several paintings in it; some are big, some are small. People did them and they are here now. I believe after this is over, they will be hung in government buildings. Why the government is involved in an art show is beyond me. I also think it is pointless for a human to paint scenes of nature when they could go outside and stand in it. Anyway, please do not misinterpret the fact that I am talking right now as genuine interest in art and attempt to discuss it with me further. End of speech."[87]

No manager, coach, or president can motivate those within their organization or country unless they themselves are inspired by their work. Ron acts as a leader who genuinely cares for those he works with but fails to build up members in his community. By showing how little he cares about the art, he makes it clear that he would accept – and even encourage – their lack of effort.

Leaders may not understand how to sway enthusiasm or commitment to inspire people, which is a regular obstacle for those entering positions of power. It's worth remembering that, with words and actions alike, those in leadership roles can easily dishearten or embolden others. Those who take the time to inspire their organization will become the individuals who are remembered after they are gone.

Alexander the Great, Lord of Asia

Alexander the Great was king of the ancient Macedonia Empire and one of history's greatest military minds. He started his prolific military career at the age of 16 when his father sent him to lead the country's army into battle against Thebes. The opposing army was thought to be one of the most feared in the world at the time, making this a daunting task for any commander, especially for a boy in his first battle. Alexander proved his bravery to his men and secured the victory when he led the cavalry attack into the select forces, the Sacred Band of Thebes.[88]

At the age of 20, Alexander became king of Macedonia following the assassination of his father. He worked quickly, getting rid of his political rivals and securing his title as their country's leader. He pushed for further expansion of Macedonia, pursuing what seemed like an impossible dream of conquering all of Asia.[88] It didn't take long before fame of the young warrior king spread across the ancient world.

The Battle of Gaugamela was one of Alexander's most legendary conflicts, for that victory assured his legacy, giving him control of the Persian Empire. In the clash, Alexander faced a Persian army double the size of his own.[89] Despite the grim outlook, neither Alexander nor his men faltered; they held the confidence of a team who believed in their leader's skills.

The Persians tried to outflank and surround Alexander. In committing so strongly to this tactic, the Persian army left the center of their battle line exposed, which Alexander took advantage of to guide his personal cavalry into enemy forces. This puncture sent the Persian forces into chaos as they tried to retreat. They were ultimately unsuccessful and lost 20,000 of their 100,000 men. Alexander, however, won the battle with losing only 700 of his 47,000 forces.[90]

During his 13-year reign, Alexander never lost a single battle. This was not just due to his military acumen, but to the loyalty of his men. He repeatedly inspired his soldiers to overcome whatever adversary they came against, propelling them to follow his command almost blindly since they saw he was just as willing to give his life.

Leaders must have conviction for the causes which they draw others into. They can inspire their people to face upcoming challenges through their own personal attitude and actions. Luckily, there is no single "right path" those in leadership can take to best convince others to follow. This stems back to your personal beliefs and your willingness to show authenticity to your team. It takes a leader being consistently genuine to build that bond with their staff. Once you obtain that devotion, there's no limit to what your organization can achieve.

Maintain Control Through Chaos

Every organization experiences setbacks. Ultimately, it's up to leaders to bring a sense of calm and control to these difficult situations. Those who fail to be pillars of resolve for their organizations in times of need run the risk of sending their team into chaos. People need reassurance there's no reason to fear.

The Skipper Always Knows What to Do

In the 2000 movie *U-571*, Americans send the S-33 submarine on a covert mission to capture the Enigma cipher machine from a damaged German U-boat named the U-571. The sought-after device is what the German Army uses to send coded messages to each of their remotely-deployed units. The Americans believe if they are able to capture this machine, they will be able to intercept their communications and be one step closer to ending the war.

The plan is for a team led by Lt. Tyler – the S-33's executive officer (XO) – to board U-571 disguised as a German rescue team and secure the Enigma. He is second in command, and, while he does not have covert operations experience, Tyler is someone the men can trust. The operation is a success. But as they prepare to transport the Enigma and the team back to the S-33, they are spotted by a German Destroyer. Before they can get back safely, the Destroyer sinks the S-33, leaving the team stranded on the open water. Lt. Tyler and his small team retreat into U-571 and dive to avoid meeting the same fate as the rest of their crew.

Once they escape the reach of the German Destroyer, the U-571 fires a torpedo. This not only sinks the opponents' ship, but prevents anyone from learning of the takeover. Although they are safe from immediate danger, Lt. Tyler's squad finds itself in enemy waters in a damaged ship with the stolen Enigma cipher machine. There is understandable panic, and the men look to Lt. Tyler for guidance. He is just as clueless and equally as nervous as the rest of them, so he explodes and reveal that he has no idea how to get them home. Immediately after, the chief – a senior enlisted member from the S-33 – pulls Lt. Tyler aside and gives him much-needed advice:

> This is the Navy, where a commanding officer is a mighty and terrible thing; a man to be feared and respected, all knowing, all powerful. Don't you dare say what you said to the boys back there again, 'I don't know.' Those three words will kill a crew, dead as a depth charge. You're the skipper now, and the skipper always knows what to do whether he does or not.[91]

The chief understands that, as the leader, Lt. Tyler has to compose himself and show strength for the sake of the team. Leadership is tested most when organizations have to face forces beyond their control. During those instances, it's a leader's responsibility to set the example. If they keep their cool during adversity, it gives hope to onlookers that everything is going to be all right.

My AMU had a temporary duty mission (TDY) for a week in California to assist pilots in training on open-sea flights. Along with the chief, I led this endeavor, taking 50 of our airmen while the rest remained at the base. We were at a high tempo of sortie generation while on TDY, and our airmen rose to the occasion. Through the first few days, we were able to launch the aircraft and get them ready without any issues.

While away from the home station, we received awful news that one of the airmen who worked as a weapons troop back at Luke AFB had committed suicide early one morning. Many knew this individual personally. I was scared this information would upset and distract some of my guys from their work, which – in aircraft maintenance – is a dangerous prospect. If you're distracted while working on the flight line, one mistake can get you, another maintainer, or even the pilot killed.

With this in mind, I hosted an AMU meeting before the morning shift and started off by telling them the grave news about the airman. I offered condolence to those who were friends with him and made it clear that if anyone wanted to take some time off to talk to me or anyone else, there would be no questions from supervisors. Still, it was my duty to drive home the last point. If they were out on the flight line, they owed it to each other and the pilots to make sure they were focused and did their jobs properly.

I'm not sure if what I said that day had any lasting impact on the airmen. But I do know that we finished the week without any incidents and performed as efficiently as we ever had. That moment helped me understand more about my responsibility as a leader in the AMU. It went beyond making sure that we had the aircraft on schedule; I also needed to be there for my people when the emotional challenges presented themselves.

A Citadel of Freedom

Another example of maintaining control through words of encouragement is how King George VI rallied his citizens around a message of positivity during war. By 1940, Hitler had quickly worked his way through Europe, adding country after country to the growing empire of the Third Reich until he reached the sea. Hitler looked to bring the United Kingdom to its knees by organizing a massive and prolonged bombing campaign. These air raids started in 1940 and lasted for a year.

Shortly before the bombings began, the British government suggested that King George VI and his family flee to Canada to ensure their safety. The king refused; he understood that, during this dark time, the British people needed to see their ruler stand by them. He wanted to reassure his citizens that all was not lost and that they would get through this adversity together. On September 23, just 16 days into the London Blitz, King George VI shared a radio address with his countrymen from an air raid bunker underneath Buckingham Palace. In this speech, he reassured his public of their strength and asked the nation to endure the attacks:

> The walls of London may be battered, but the spirit of the Londoner stands resolute and undismayed. As in London, so throughout Great Britain, buildings rich in beauty and historic interest may be wantonly attacked and humble homes no less dear and familiar may be destroyed. But there'll always be an England to stand before the world as a symbol and a citadel of freedom.[92]

The king understood that, in challenging moments, the most dangerous thing people could lose was hope. Because of his resolve, King George VI became a symbol of British pride and strength during WWII. Leaders who guide others through shared hardships without losing composure gain the trust and loyalty of their people.

Trickle-Down Attitude Reflection Questions

- What's your normal attitude when around the people in your organization? Are you generally upbeat, angry, morose, or even emotionless?
- Now consider the normal mindset/behavior of your team when you're around them. What's it like?

Recognize the Contributions of Your People

- How does the recognition of achievements change the attitude of an organization?
- How do you publicly recognize the contributions of your team members to their peers?

Inspire Your Organization to Push Through Challenges

- What leaders (those you worked under personally or just observed) inspired you in your life? How did they do it?
- Why is it the responsibility of a leader to inspire their people? Why can they not self-motivate?
- If you worked on your own team, do you think you'd be inspired by your own leadership? Why or why not?

Maintain Control Through Chaos

- If you were to lose your cool in a stressful situation, how would your people react?
- Have you had "moments of crisis" while you've been in a leadership position? If so, how did you handle them? Is there anything you'd change upon looking back?

8

LIVE YOUR PRINCIPLES

Professional development is an aspect the Air Force takes seriously for both its officers and enlisted individuals. Once a month, we held Officer Mentorship Meetings in the maintenance group to help us hone our skillset. Senior officers taught juniors about military history, maintenance best practices, or career progression. In one particular gathering, Col. Jacobs shared the importance of doing what you believe is right even if it hurts your career.

When Col. Jacobs was a major, he had been assigned command of the Aircraft Maintenance Squadron (AMXS). He was energetic and dedicated to making sure his squadron was the best in the group; in fact, he even brought his radio when he went home for dinner, so he could be aware of what was going on in his squadron's flights while away. Because of his in-touch leadership, he was seen as a "fast burner," someone whose high performance moved them up the ranks quicker than normal.

One day, Maj. Jacobs was called into his group commander's office for mentoring on how to best move forward in his career. His commander told him he was impressed with Maj. Jacobs's work ethic and wanted to fulfill his potential in the Air Force by walking him through everything he needed to do in order to become a general. Maj. Jacobs was honored and excited to be praised by his commander. But, as the discussion progressed, Maj. Jacobs noticed many of the tasks were extracurricular to his primary job. This meant taking on these additional responsibilities would cause him to lose involvement with his current squad. Maj. Jacobs relayed his reservations to his group commander about spending so much time outside of his everyday duties. His group commander understood the major's apprehension, but told him that this was the way things worked and if he didn't take part in these extra tasks, then he would never become a general. After weighing his options, Maj. Jacobs ultimately decided he would not be comfortable spreading himself so thin and not giving his people his best effort.

Col. Jacobs confirmed that the decision to *not* take on those additional responsibilities prevented him from progressing in rank as quickly (and ultimately meant he would never be in consideration for general). He made peace with this and said he held no regrets with how he spent his career. He emphasized that the point of his story was not that it was bad to take on duties outside of primary ones or to progress quickly in rank, but that there was more significance in living out one's principles.

In a world that is increasingly focused on results, principled leadership can sometimes seem unnecessary. The truth is when a leader has values that they make known and commit to living and leading by those values it has an effect on those within their organization. To be a two-part leader, you must be someone your people respect and want to follow. They have to want to follow your example, not just your orders.

You Are the Face of Your Organization

A leader must incorporate and act on their principles because their values influence their being. After all, they are the face of their organization. Leadership represents their team in everything they say or do. People from inside and out often judge an entire organization based on the actions of its leaders. This comes with a lot of power; people in these roles can easily build or destroy the notoriety of their department in how they behave.

MISSION FIRST, PEOPLE ALWAYS

Door-to-Door Sales

Shark Tank is a business-related reality TV series in which entrepreneurs pitch their struggling ventures before five industry titans (also known as "sharks"). If the sharks are interested in investing, they'll offer money for equity in the company. These individuals only have a couple of minutes to choose to invest – and, in so many cases, the decision is based equally on how they feel about the CEO that is pitching as well as their sales numbers.

In a 2013 episode of the series, the sharks immediately expressed interest in Mission Belt and its CEO. Nate Holzapfel entered the shark tank with boundless energy, showing the sharks his company's modification on the common belt. The $39,000 worth of sales for Mission Belt were promising for the three months he had been in operation, but this didn't blow the sharks away.[93] What impressed them more than the product was when Nate told them that, upon arriving in L.A. for the show the previous night, he had decided to use his free time to go door to door, selling his product. This commitment and work ethic convinced Daymond John, a shark on the panel and the founder of FUBU, to back Mission Belt on the condition that Nate would continue to be in charge of all sales for the company.

After appearing on *Shark Tank*, Mission Belt's sales skyrocketed, earning $1 million of revenue in a single month. While people sought the actual items, like the sharks, they also responded to Nate himself and how he presented his company. They bought into his positivity, his energy, and his mission (which promises one dollar of every sale to microloans for entrepreneurs in Third World countries).[91] In creating this brand and asserting its value, Nate helped investors and customers understand his company was about more than an accessory.

Leaders who envision themselves as ambassadors of their organizations rather than just caretakers inspire endorsement from both inside and out of the company. Nate understood that the sharks were not buying Mission Belt; they were buying him as a leader. This responsibility forces leaders to be aware of the public perception they put out. Anything inappropriate or hypocritical reflects poorly on those they oversee.

Live Your Principles

Heir Apparent

At the height of the French Revolution in August of 1792, King Louis XVI and his family were taken from the Tuileries Palace in Paris and imprisoned. A few months later, he and his wife, Marie Antoinette, were found guilty of treason and executed by way of the guillotine. This left their eldest son, Louis Charles XVII, in line for the throne if the monarchy were to ever regain power.[94] In a sermon entitled *The King's Son,* Bishop Vaughn J. Featherstone shares a story about Louis Charles XVII, the boy who French royalists called the King of France even while he was imprisoned:

Many years ago, I heard the story of the son of King Louis XVI of France. King Louis had been taken from his throne and imprisoned. His young son, the prince, was taken by those who dethroned the king. They thought that inasmuch as the king's son was heir to the throne, if they could destroy him morally, he would never realize the great and grand destiny that life had bestowed upon him.

> They took him to a community far away, and there they exposed the lad to every filthy and vile thing that life could offer. They exposed him to foods the richness of which would quickly make him a slave to appetite. They used vile language around him constantly. They exposed him to lewd and lusting women. They exposed him to dishonor and distrust. He was surrounded 24 hours a day by everything that could drag the soul of a man as low as one could slip. For over six months, he had this treatment – but not once did the young lad buckle under pressure.
>
> Finally, after intensive temptation, they questioned him. Why had he not submitted himself to these things – why had he not partaken? These things would provide pleasure, satisfy his lusts, and were desirable; they were all

his. The boy said, "I cannot do what you ask for I was born to be a king.⁹⁵

Even as a child, Louis Charles XVII understood the responsibility he had to the people of France. If the monarchy were able to retake the throne, he would be responsible for guiding a country that had just gone through revolution. Louis Charles XVII prepared himself to be the face of a nation, but he knew he couldn't take on that role successfully if he did not live his life of captivity in accordance with the royal principles he had been taught. Leaders who discern the implications of their personal actions on their organization will set themselves and their people up for success.

Your Every Move Is Observed

Those in leadership roles may think their actions only impact themselves, that how they go about their daily activities has no bearing on their organization, but this is false. Team members watch everything their leader does, looking for insight into what they're thinking. Often, a leader can send unintended messages depending on their actions.

Presidential Politics

This is especially true for our government leaders in the age of social media and the 24-hour news cycle. There are people who base their entire careers on breaking down the actions, words, and body language of our political leaders to decipher their true intentions. Such scrutiny by the American people now plays an active role in our understanding of politics. It pressures those in power to be hypervigilant of how their comments and mannerisms come off; any deviation from positive connotations has the potential to lose the support of their staff and the public.

The 1992 Presidential Election was a close contest between Republican incumbent President George H. W. Bush and Democrat challenger Governor Bill Clinton, with Ross Perot running as an Independent. During national election campaigns, candidates hold televised debates, thus giving them the opportunity to share their goals with the American people all at once. It was in one of these conversations that President Bush made a seemingly insignificant action that ended up speaking volumes.

A member of the audience asked how the national debt personally affected each of the candidates, and President Bush checked his watch while answering the question. Such a simple act sent the message to the public that he didn't care about the debate and had more important things to do. Whether any of that was true or not, President Bush demonstrated indifference during a pivotal moment and faltered by not being aware of the implications of his mannerisms.[96] George H. W. Bush lost the election to Bill Clinton, an anomaly for an incumbent president running for reelection. This loss was due to many factors, but one of the primary reasons was that people believed Clinton cared more about them.[97]

I'm sure George H. W. Bush cared about the questions and concerns of average Americans, but he was not mindful of his actions. It is important to be aware that those in leadership roles are constantly communicating using what they say, post, and do. Sometimes, without speaking so much as a word, a leader can endorse or condemn ideas and behaviors. This makes it more important for them to be deliberate in their actions and to match what they claim to believe.

A Battle Worth Fighting

In Harper Lee's 1960 novel *To Kill a Mockingbird*, in which Atticus Finch – a small-town lawyer, local leader in Maycomb, and single father to two children, Jem and Scout – helps his fellow residents understand the injustice of African-Americans. This, of course, is set during the Jim Crow era, which meant tension already ran high. Atticus tries to use whatever influence he has to send a positive message to both the community and his children about the importance of equality for all.

MISSION FIRST, PEOPLE ALWAYS

An important opportunity comes for him with the trial of Tom Robinson, a Black man accused of raping a White woman. At that time in Alabama, a simple accusation of such was the same as the death penalty. Atticus agrees to defend Tom without thinking twice despite the odds being stacked against him. He wanted to take on the impossible task of showing how a Black man could receive a fair trial in the South.

As the case progresses, the courtroom becomes packed with those in support of the defendant and those who just want to see how Atticus will prove the man's innocence. The case builds slowly as Atticus meticulously dissects each part of the allegations against Tom, verifying every detail. Those in the courtroom soon grow frustrated with Atticus's slow pace of confirming and reconfirming how the attack was said to have taken place.

Eventually, it becomes clear what Atticus has been building toward as he brings forth his primary defense evidence – the assailant had to have been left-handed. This is a significant fact because Tom only had the use of his right arm. Understanding the gravity of this discovery forces those in the court to sit in a stunned silence. Tom Robinson is innocent.

In the end, however, it doesn't matter because the jury finds Tom guilty of the crime. Regardless of Atticus' hard work, the trial produces the expected result. He explains that people are not ready yet to accept the idea of equal rights. Jem angrily questions Atticus, saying if he knew that he wasn't going to win, what was the point of even trying.

Atticus responds with an impactful message: "I wanted you to see what real courage is, instead of getting the idea that courage is a man with a gun in his hand. It's when you know you're licked before you begin, but you begin anyway and see it through no matter what."[98]

Atticus understood if equality was ever going to be achieved, it was going to take community leaders like himself forging a path. He used that influence to not only teach his children about standing up for what is right, but to demonstrate that, regardless of race, people deserve to be treated as innocent until proved guilty. While Tom did not receive justice, his trial revealed to the town what their elected official, Atticus, believed.

Once those in power realize their people pay attention to what they do, they choose what messages they broadcast. If leaders want to leave an impression on the people in their organization, they need to be intentional with the words they use and the actions they take. They then inspire and motivate others to perform at a higher level.

Your Personal Character Matters

Society often builds up past leaders as being beyond moral reproach, as something we should aspire to live up to. This is the same with heart-touching and strong protagonists in film and literature; everyone wants to follow a top-notch character, someone who exemplifies their principles. It is not a leader's responsibility to be perfect all of the time, but they do have to back up their values in order to motivate those within their organization.

Scandal in the Deep South

Consider Jeff Sessions, the U.S. Senator from Alabama who vacated his Senate seat to become the U.S. Attorney General in 2017. The state held a special election later that year to fill Senator Session's open seat and, after a close primary, the citizens had the choice between Republican candidate Roy Moore and Democratic candidate Doug Jones.

This seemed like a slam dunk for Roy Moore, who was about as conservative a candidate as you could get in a state that had not elected a Democratic Senator since 1991. He held all the popular policy views of most people in the state: He was pro-life, pro-second amendment, pro-states' rights, and deeply religious.[99] Judge Moore even had some notoriety in the state because, fourteen years earlier, he had been removed as a chief justice of the Alabama

Supreme Court for refusing to clear away a statue of the Ten Commandments from in front of the state courthouse.[100] This made Judge Moore a hero among conservatives, and it seemed that the Republican Party was going to keep its stronghold in the South.

Not too long after campaigning had begun however, allegations against Judge Moore surfaced, claiming that – while working in the district attorney's office as a full-time prosecutor in his early 30s – he had had inappropriate relationships with at least three young women ranging from the ages of 14 to 18.[101] Although none of the women accused Judge Moore of having intercourse with them as minors, the idea of an adult man being romantically involved with teenage girls was difficult for the public to ignore. The Moore campaign denied these stories, but it was clear from the polling that the allegations had impacted voters.

On Tuesday, December 12, 2017, Doug Jones won the special election in Alabama with 49.9% of the vote to Roy Moore's 48.4%.[102] In one of the closest Alabama senate races in the last three decades, the voters had made a statement of what kind of character they expected from their leaders. Even those who disagreed with the policies that Doug Jones represented voted for him because they did not question his morals.

People frequently place their leaders on imaginary pedestals in believing they have the integrity to withstand adversity that would take down others. When those in leadership make it clear that they aren't living up to those standards, they lose people's support.

The Prince of Peace

Jesus of Nazareth was a simple carpenter when he started his ministry at the age of 30. He was no one of great influence nor had he achieved any great feats. As shown in Matthew 13:55, even his own community questioned him when he announced that he was the promised Messiah the Jewish people had been waiting for. The people asked, "Is this not the carpenter's son?" They scoffed at the idea that Jesus, whom they had known their entire lives, could be anything more than the son of a carpenter.

He was met with the same skepticism by those who would end up being his most devoted followers. In John 1:46, Nathanael, one of his 12 apostles, asks, "Can there any good thing come out of Nazareth?"

Within three years, Jesus developed from relative obscurity to one of the most influential teachers in the world. Beyond that, many followed Jesus because of who he was, which was unlike other religious leaders who, as scholars, were fixated on maintaining power in the community rather than in helping individuals within it.

Other religious guides tried to unmask Jesus as a fraud and show people that he could not be the Messiah, but these attempts failed and only increased people's reverence. Jesus utilized these opportunities not only to show followers how they were supposed to behave, but to call out the hypocrisy of their current leadership.

Even after Jesus's death, his followers spread his teachings around the world to bring the Gospel of Jesus Christ to those who needed His peace. Today, Christianity is the world's largest religion with 2.3 billion followers.[103]

People expect integrity and character in the those they work for or follow. They want to believe their leaders are good people who practice what they preach because it shows their values can transcend into their work. When leaders live up to that expectation, they win the loyalty of those in their organization.

Dependability Is the Basis of Trust

When organizations believe their leaders are individuals of high character and sound judgment, they're more likely to trust the decisions they make, even if they don't agree with all of them. People who show strong work ethic, positive attitude, dependability, and unwavering support for their people earn respect because of their credentials as well as who they have shown themselves to be.

MISSION FIRST, PEOPLE ALWAYS

The Boy Who Lived

The *Harry Potter* book series explores the life and adventures of the titular character, Harry Potter, a teenage wizard who attends Hogwarts School of Witchcraft and Wizardry. He is no ordinary wizard, for he survived an attack by Voldemort, a dark lord, as a baby. This miraculous survival not only makes Harry an instant legend in the magical world but puts him in harm's way of Voldemort's supporters.

During Harry's brushes with danger, he relies on help from his friends, Ron Weasley, Hermione Granger, and Albus Dumbledore, the headmaster of Hogwarts. Dumbledore is known as the most powerful wizard in the world; in fact, he is the only one Voldemort fears. The headmaster takes particular interest in Harry and his development and offers guidance and support in Harry's darkest times.

The final book of the series begins with a bleak picture: Voldemort regains power and tightens his grip once again upon the wizarding world. Following Dumbledore's sudden death, Harry is left with the assignment to track down and destroy the five remaining Horcruxes (cursed items imbued with fragments of Voldemort's soul) and destroy the Dark Lord once and for all. It seems Dumbledore has sent Harry on an impossible mission, and the boy hasn't any idea where such items could be. The only clue he has is that they are things Voldemort has considered important.

As Harry and his friends near the end of their mission, they request the help of Aberforth Dumbledore, the headmaster's younger brother. Unfortunately, Aberforth hated his brother and believed that he did not deserve Harry's loyalty.

Harry Potter: We need to get into Hogwarts, tonight. Dumbledore gave us a job to do.

Aberforth Dumbledore: Did he now? Nice job? Easy?

Harry Potter: We've been hunting Horcruxes. We think the last one's inside the castle, but we'll need your help in getting in.

Live Your Principles

Aberforth Dumbledore: It's not a job my brother's given you. It's a suicide mission. Do yourself a favor, boy, and go home. Live a little longer.

Harry Potter: Dumbledore trusted me to see this through.

Aberforth Dumbledore: What makes you think you can trust him? What makes you think you can believe anything my brother told you? In all the time you knew him, did he ever mention my name?

Harry Potter: Why should he –

Aberforth Dumbledore: Keep secrets? You tell me.

Harry Potter: I trusted him.

Aberforth Dumbledore: That's a boy's answer. A boy who goes chasing Horcruxes on the word of a man who wouldn't even tell you where to start. You're lying! Not just to me, it doesn't matter, but to yourself as well. That's what a fool does. You don't strike me as a fool, Harry Potter. So, I'll ask you again, there must be a reason.

Harry Potter: I'm not interested in what happened between you and your brother. I don't care that you've given up. I trusted the man I knew. We need to get into the castle tonight.[104]

Harry trusts that, even though he received no help, Dumbledore had a reason for asking him to complete this mission the way he did. The faith and loyalty Harry shows Dumbledore comes from how he's seen the late headmaster make decisions that protected those in his school and the wizarding world over the last six years.

Leaders who demonstrate admirable character to their people through consistent and dependable choices will easily build trust. Everyone wants to follow an individual upon whom they can rely. When it's revealed that a leader cannot live up to expectations, they lose empathy from their people and cannot effectively lead.

Management consulting company Gallup has conducted national polls annually about how much confidence Americans place in different institutions since the 1970s. These include small businesses, the medical sector, news media, congress, police, and the supreme court. Since the polling began, the American public has voted the military as the establishment they trust most by a wide margin.[105] Those voting believe there is something that sets the military and its members apart from the rest of society. They perceive troops and those who command them as individuals who live by a code of honor at times when it is difficult to.

Thinking Man's General

In this world of honorable men and women leading their people, General David Petraeus stood out from the rest. He served as the commander of the U.S. and International Security Assistance Forces (ISAF) in Afghanistan as well Commander of U.S. Central Command during a time when the Operation Iraqi Freedom was in chaos. General Petraeus was often referred to as the "thinking man's general," due to his Ph.D. from Princeton and how he was willing to break the mold in how he approached campaign strategies.[106] This tendency to think in a different way than other military leaders helped the general as he went on to create and implement the strategy responsible for turning around Operation Iraqi Freedom.

During his time serving in the Army, General Petraeus was renowned for his commitment to honesty and transparency; he was known to operate by the mantra "Be first with the truth"[107] while serving in positions of leadership. He believed the more transparency his organizations worked under, the better they would be able to work with others and serve the American people. For this reason, General Petraeus was always direct and comfortable with the media as the Commander of the U.S. Central Command.

Live Your Principles

This is why the nation was shocked to discover that Director Petraeus was accused of not only infidelity, but of leaking top-secret information to his mistress, Paula Broadwell. She was a former army intelligence officer who was, at the time of the affair, working on the director's biography. Director Petraeus gave Miss Broadwell access to his personal notebooks that contained classified information. The reaction to this breach of both personal and professional conduct was instant and, less than a week after the news of his misconduct broke, Director Petraeus was called to the Oval Office where he gave his letter of resignation to the president.[104]

While David Petraeus had proved himself a man of superior talent and excellent character over his many decades of service, his affair erased his earned military reputation. His character and integrity were called into question so much that it created a lack of confidence in his ability to successfully lead. By virtue of their positions, leaders are held to a high standard. When they are caught falling short and do not show the character their people expect, it is difficult for them to continue to lead.

As the decision-makers for an organization, people in power have a strong influence on the professional and personal futures of their team members. Leaders must be dependable not to do the most advantageous or popular thing, but the *right* thing. While individuals in an organization know their leader is not perfect, they still want to trust he or she is a principled individual. If they cannot trust leaders to live up to their own basic standards, then how can they be expected to trust them with weightier matters, like their livelihood?

Decide What Principles Will Influence Your Organization's Culture

Leaders indirectly affect those in their organization by the ways they uphold and live their principles. They are also responsible for creating and influencing the culture of their organization by determining the principles they find most important. Leaders who do not take this duty seriously lose an opportunity to impact their team in a meaningful way. Culture shapes their organization's productivity while simultaneously boosting their people's morale.

A One-Way Conversation

Near the end of my senior year of ROTC, my class and I prepared to graduate and enter the Air Force as officers. Although we had practiced our leadership among each other, we were a little nervous to learn how our experiences would translate to active duty. Each of us fell somewhere on the spectrum between terrified and ecstatic at the prospect of being looked to as a leader with real authority by airmen who wanted as much guidance as possible beforehand.

Our instructor, Col. Green, recognized how we felt, having gone through the same process when he was commissioning into the Air Force. He also understood – after years of teaching us – our potential as leaders. Col. Green served in multiple positions of leadership and knew the impact we would have on our organizations if we had the confidence to boldly implement our principles. Because he wanted us to be well-adjusted, Col. Green relayed a story from his career that helped him realize the impact he could have as a leader.

As a squadron commander, then-Lt. Col. Green held a quarterly awards ceremony with the entire squadron in attendance. Everything proceeded as normal with airmen and officers coming to the front to be recognized for the superb work they accomplished over the last quarter. Then, as a female airman came to the stage, someone from the audience yelled, "Finally, some eye candy!"

There was some laughter from the audience, but one person who did not think this was a joke was Lt. Col. Green. He paused the event and instructed the individual who made the comment to see him in his office immediately afterwards.

As Lt. Col. Green entered his office, he found a very scared airman waiting for him. As he sat behind his desk, the airmen blurted out an explanation for his actions. Lt. Col. Green cut him off and informed him that he did not care about reasons or excuses; this was not going to be a conversation, but a much-needed lesson. The message had to be sent to this airman, as well as others in the squadron, that inappropriate behavior was not acceptable in public or in private – that everyone in the squadron deserved the same respect, irrespective of their gender, race, sexual preference, or religious views.

By calling out the comment in front of the entire squadron, Lt. Col. Green defined his expectation of their unit culture. Leaders who decide what the culture of their organization will be, instead of letting it develop on its own, hold a stronger grasp on the safety and morale of their people. As everyone understands and assimilates to the culture of an organization, it will help them know what is appropriate and what is tolerated.

MISSION FIRST, PEOPLE ALWAYS

Live Your Principles Reflection Questions

- Are you aware of how you present yourself within your organization? How about how you express yourself to those outside of it?
- What can you personally do to improve the perception of your organization?

Your Every Move Is Observed

- What message do you believe your actions send out?
- What messages do you want your people to take away from your daily actions and attitude?
- Are there any alternative behaviors you can implement in your daily routine to send the messages you want?

Your Personal Character Matters

- Is there a discrepancy between how you present yourself publicly and how you conduct yourself privately?
- If so, how do you think it would affect the way people view you if that covert behavior became public knowledge?

Dependability Is the Basis of Trust

- Do you and your people share mutual trust? If you do, write down a few reasons why that trust exists. If not, why?
- Have you done anything that, if uncovered, would cause those in your organization to scrutinize the decisions you make?

Decide What Principles Will Influence Your Organization's Culture

- What principles make up the culture of your organization?
- In what ways do you enforce these principles?

9

GET TO KNOW YOUR PEOPLE

    In the aircraft maintenance career field, TDYs are opportunities for officers to develop their leadership skills outside of the familiar operations of their home stations. A leader's responsibilities required to prepare for a TDY range from logistics planning for supplies to personnel management to leading airmen in completing their assigned mission.

    My first TDY came when I was a lieutenant; I took 100 of my enlisted airmen and 12 of our aircraft from Luke AFB to Miramar MCAS in San Diego. This mission was to support our flying squadron in completing valuable training exercises over the ocean. Back at the base, I assisted my OIC in ensuring the mission was complete but always had him as my safety net if anything were to go wrong. As the leader on this TDY, I alone was responsible for all the people and equipment.

    This extra pressure initially closed me off from everyone else on the TDY. Instead of spending time with my people, I isolated myself, spent my free time frantically checking (and double-checking) things I knew were already finished, and became irritable with those around me. TDYs were ordinarily a time where people drew closer to each other because they only had each other to rely on, but my attitude expanded the distance between me and my airmen.

One day about halfway through the TDY, I noticed a group of my airmen tossing a football around while waiting for pilots to return from their mission. As I watched them talking and laughing together, I made the choice to put my worries aside and join them. They were surprised to see me lowering my guard and joking with them, but that afternoon enabled me to take a break from the stress and create a connection with my people.

From that point on, my experience on the TDY changed. I was able to better relate to and lead my airmen as I got to know them individually. I spent my free time among the airmen, chatting and trusting them to do their jobs instead of micromanaging. In turn, they trusted me more, updating me on what issues they faced (including the ones they did not feel like they could ask me for support for originally). This mutual trust fed into smooth operations that provided enough aircraft to complete our mission days ahead of schedule.

Leaders are unable to accomplish anything great by themselves; they need the full support of their people if they want to be successful. Those who truly become two-part leaders step outside of their comfort zone to get to know their people and build a connection that goes beyond policies and procedures. This effort and vulnerability not only will earn the respect of those within an organization, but give a leader valuable insight into the individuals they oversee.

Make the Effort to Build Relationships

The confidence that comes with building a relationship can't grow from nothing, which is why those in positions of power must make a concentrated effort to talk to their people and foster trust. This will take different forms depending on the person and the industry they work in, but it needs to involve sincerity. Without any attempt on the leader's part to forge this mutual trust, the staff will most likely view their leadership as faceless enforcers and nothing more.

Get to Know Your People

Walking a Mile in Their Shoes

The TV show *Undercover Boss* (2010-2017) follows leaders of corporations as they disguise themselves and experience low-level jobs within their companies. These leaders feel that if they are disguised, they'll be more likely to understand the issues their employees face on a daily basis. Many executives take this opportunity to ask their staff how they feel about the leadership of their organization and if they feel valued. Since these conversations promote unfiltered opinions about the operation, bosses can receive firsthand evaluations on how to improve their management.

One of those bosses was Todd Pederson, the president and CEO of Vivint, Inc., a home security and energy company. Mr. Pederson joined some of his ground-level employees disguised as Eddie, a budding entrepreneur trying to learn how a successful company functions. While in character, Mr. Pederson spoke to his employees and performed their duties, which included experiencing the obstacles everyday workers face. These struggles ranged from difficulties at work due to company policies to trials in their personal lives. The issues were specific to each of the individuals he worked with, but the common thread was that they did not have a relationship of trust with leadership. They did not believe he cared about their wellbeing as humans or employees.

After spending time undercover with multiple employees, Mr. Pederson confessed, "I've tried to be a leader with the intention of taking care of the people inside of Vivint. Am I doing that as effectively as possible? I didn't really feel like that every single time I was out on these job sites. That is probably the thing that has bothered me the most because that is my fault."[108]

When the time came for Mr. Pederson to reveal himself as the CEO, he made sure to make it count. He did not want to waste his chance to build trust with the people he had worked with nor waste his opportunity with the rest of his company to show what kind of leader he was. The first step he took was overhauling processes that made jobs more difficult for his employees, including supplying upgraded safety equipment for his technicians; revamping his warehouses inventory, scheduling; ordering systems; and even providing immersion training for all salesmen. On top of that, Mr. Pederson sat down with each of the individuals he worked with and committed to helping them with their personal obstacles by giving over $250,000 of his own money to help with personal debt, court fees, children's education, and medical expenses.[106]

    Todd Pederson put forth the effort to learn not just about the operations in his organization but about the people who run them. In doing so, he exhibited to all that he was as a leader who cared about their wellbeing. As leaders reach out to individuals they don't directly work with and listen to their thoughts, ideas, and concerns, they will understand more about their organization and any unnoticed problems. This insight will, in turn, help staff members obtain a stronger sense of who they're following and understand why they deserve their loyalty.

Swing-Shift Stopovers

    Squadron commanders in a maintenance group are usually in their position for 12 to 18 months, so welcoming a new individual to this role is not an uncommon event. The new squadron commander usually schedules an all-call meeting where they introduce themselves to the entire squadron. They pop around various flights over the next couple of weeks to get acquainted with their people and the work they're doing. These short visits are a way for a new squadron commander to let the airmen know who they are on a more personal level. While these visits are appreciated, they aren't frequent enough to make any lasting impact.

    When Maj. Henderson was announced as our new AMXS commander, I expected more of the same formalities. I was shocked when – one night as I was working the night shift a week after Maj. Henderson took over – I walked into the AMU breakroom and found him joking around with some airmen.

Never had I seen one of my senior leaders interacting with the maintainers in such a casual way, nor had I known a squadron commander to swing by to my unit unannounced without my airmen formed up and ready to properly receive them.

After stumbling in on their conversation, I immediately apologized to Maj. Henderson for not having the AMU prepped for his arrival. He pulled me aside and explained to me that he decided to come in for the night shifts for a week or two and walk around that way he could meet maintainers who he would probably not be able to talk with under normal circumstances. He also instructed me not to alert any of the leadership of any other AMU that he was going to be stopping by their units; it was important to Maj. Henderson that he could engage with the airmen as naturally as possible without their AMU leadership looking over their shoulders.

These swing-shift stopovers had a huge impact. Spending time with the maintainers in their environment did more to build trust with the airmen in the squadron than any number of speeches, briefings, or new policies could ever accomplish. The men and women responded positively as word spread. Even airmen who had not actually seen Maj. Henderson out on the flight line or in the AMU offices were excited to follow him upon hearing how much he cared.

People want to be able to trust their leaders. They want to believe their leaders have their best interests at heart by earning it as Maj. Henderson did. Leaders must work to earn this connection and not expect it to be freely given.

Your people respond to leadership as trust blooms; they will feel more comfortable to come to their leader with issues or suggestions. The insights you gain form a stronger relationship with those you lead which will help you create an environment where your people can be more satisfied with their work.

MISSION FIRST, PEOPLE ALWAYS

Charging the Hill

Theodore Roosevelt was serving as the Assistant Secretary of the Navy when the U.S. entered the Spanish-American War (April 1898-December 1898). Moved by his desire to serve his country in a more active capacity, Assistant Secretary Roosevelt gave up his position in the McKinley administration and was granted a commission in the Army as a lieutenant colonel. The first assignment he received was leading a specialized unit of frontiersmen who were qualified as expert riders and marksmen. These men – who history would know as the Rough Riders – were deployed to the front lines in Cuba. The members of the unit were selected from all around the country, acting as a microcosm of the nation. Within five days of the announcement of LTC Roosevelt assembling a team, over 20,000 applied to fill the 800 available slots.[109] These men were excited not just about their unique mission but to serve under LTC Roosevelt, famous for toughness and ferocity in his political career. They were men who were ready to be part of something meaningful at an important time in their country's history.

As LTC Roosevelt took control of his unit, he commenced immediate action to gain the trust of his men. These were hard, seasoned individuals who respected Roosevelt for what he had accomplished already, but they would not follow him on reputation alone; he would have to earn their trust. LTC Roosevelt accomplished this by running a unit where every soldier had to prove his worth; no one got special treatment. He ate what they ate, he slept where they slept, and he even trained beside them. Before long, LTC Roosevelt had demonstrated to those in his unit how he would never ask his men to do anything he was not willing to do himself. This style of leadership was so impactful that he gained the trust and loyalty of his men.[107]

On July 1, 1898, the Rough Riders faced their greatest challenge in the Battle of San Juan Hill, which was a vital landmark to gain control of Santiago de Cuba, the country's second largest city. The U.S. forces would have to take the hill from a position that put them at a significant disadvantage. Most of the units waited at the base of the hill, nervous and scared at taking the charge into an uncertain fight.[110] LTC Roosevelt and his Rough Riders did not shirk against facing these odds; in fact, the lieutenant colonel ordered the other commanders to move out of the way so that him and his Rough Riders could close in. They faced heavy fire from enemy forces, initially pushing them back. Seeing this, LTC Roosevelt raced up from his position in the back – the traditional position for commanders – to the forefront, where he led the attack on horseback. This put himself at great risk as a primary target, but his men followed him up the hill, overwhelming the enemy and conquering the post.

The men of the Rough Riders trusted LTC Roosevelt enough to follow him directly into danger that other units were unwilling to face. His active leadership up to the Battle of San Juan Hill was instrumental in them achieving that American victory. Their heroics were not only significant in the Spanish-American War, but served as a morale boost to the Americans back home. LTC Roosevelt and the Rough Riders became icons and eventually folklore as symbols of valor.

The ability to trust their leaders helps people feel more secure with the work they do within their organization. One way this occurs is through leaders getting to know their staff and demonstrating that they care about them. Leaders have a moral and ethical responsibility to do everything they can to give their team a positive environment where they can count on security and confidence.

Find Out What Matters to Your People

Everyone wants to feel like they matter – that others are interested in what they think and care about. Leaders who take sincere interest in their people on a deeper level, such as who they are, how their lives are going, and the work that they do, will make a difference. These genuine interactions between leaders and their teams help followers feel more valued by their organizations.

The Difference a Conversation Can Make

I'm not a mechanically-minded individual, so as a new lieutenant in charge of an organization that repaired fighter jets, I often found myself confused during our production meetings. To compensate for my lack of knowledge, I decided I needed to put extra effort into talking with my airmen about repairs. Between my morning and afternoon meetings, I wandered onto the production floor to sit with my airmen, asking any question that came to mind. What fix were they performing? Why did they choose that repair over a different option? What aircraft systems did the remedy affect? What kind of training was required to complete the repair they were struggling with? Our conversations sometimes led to questions about their lives: Why did they join the Air Force? How long did they want to stay in? What did they like to do for fun?

Initially, this was something that would solely benefit myself, so I could thoroughly brief our flight's status to my leadership. I didn't even consider the impact that this time with my airmen would have on them. That was, until one day as I headed home, one of the young airmen I had worked with a couple of times over the previous week stopped me. He told me how much it meant to him that I observed and paid attention to his work; it made him feel important. He mentioned that I was the first person in his chain of command who had bothered to ask him any questions about his thoughts or interests since he had joined the Air Force a year ago. This realization was a turning point of how I interacted with my airmen going forward. I wanted to make sure they felt equally as important as that individual did.

By trying to find ways to be better prepared for my job, I stumbled onto an important leadership lesson: the significance of a leader getting out from behind their desk and getting to know their people. When team members are valued, they will do their best to live up to that and bring more success to their organization. Asking simple questions can go a long way. Leaders who take the opportunity to step out of their comfort zone and get to know the worries, challenges, and triumphs of their people will be able to build these critical connections.

Becoming a Man of the People

Franklin Delano Roosevelt, or FDR as he would be known throughout his public life, began his political aspirations in 1910 after becoming disenchanted with his first job as a lawyer. FDR found this work tedious; it did not allow him to make the impact on the world that he envisioned for himself.[109] Although he was determined to pursue a career in politics, he was unsure where to start. The Democratic political bosses ran all the local politics in those days, which is why FDR met with them to get his foothold in New York's political world.

Luckily for FDR, there was an upcoming election for a state senator in which the Democratic bosses did not have a candidate willing to run. That was because this rural district only elected a Democrat to this position once in the past 50 years. The people of the area stood in stark contrast to the metropolitan and refined world in which FDR had been raised. Jumping into the race only five weeks before the election, he knew that if he had any chance at winning, he would have to get acquainted with every voter. More than just the typical "handshake and move on," he committed to knowing them and their families, talking to them about their lives and their concerns.

FDR traveled across the district, presenting as many as 10 campaign speeches in a single day.[109] He visited people in their homes, at their places of business, and even on the road, where he stopped his car to talk to those on horseback. Even though he was an outsider in his first campaign, FDR spoke effortlessly with the citizens, becoming a welcome and trusted face in the community by listening to all of their concerns. Tom Leonard, a Democratic committeeman who worked with

FDR, recalled how the man had a talent for making those he met feel at ease, like a friend.

When the election results were released, political experts around the state were shocked to see how young FDR had willed his way to victory in the Republican stronghold. Not only had he won, but he had the greatest margin of victory of any Democratic party candidate in the state's history.[109] FDR made his people feel heard, that he cared about what happened in their lives. Despite his lack of experience or cultural differences with those in the district, they expected him to represent them in the state senate properly.

Spending time with and getting to know their people is a simple way for a leader to exhibit that they care and value their contributions. This makes individuals strive to support their leader and their vision. They gain confidence in their abilities to help their organization succeed.

Build Your People Through Mentoring

A good leader is one who creates more leaders under them. They consider the development and growth of their people as part of their team's overall success. Leaders prepare for their organization's future by actively mentoring their staff so they can be counted on to take on responsibility and help others. This is similar to the delegation chapter; you dole out tasks to others if they understand how to take ownership of a project at hand. For this to become a reality, those in charge must know who is motivated to grow in their roles and to help them reach their full potential.

Diamond in the Rough

The NBA, the premier basketball league, offers 30 head coaching positions, making these roles highly sought after and competitive. To reach this professional pinnacle, people normally must have years of experience as an NBA assistant coach, foster great success with college team or foreign league, or even be a respected NBA player. For those who fall into those categories, most never get the chance to be a head coach.

Get to Know Your People

In 2008, Erik Spoelstra was named the head coach of the Miami Heat to replace the legendary Pat Riley. With high-profile hires like that of an NBA head coach, reactions often range from excitement to outrage. For the hiring of Erik Spoelstra, the general reaction was confusion since few knew who this new coach was and why Pat Riley trusted him enough to take an administrative role with the team. What made the man who, only 10 years earlier, was the Heat's head video coordinator so special?

After finishing a brief career overseas in Germany, Coach Spoelstra's father, an NBA marketing executive, helped him find his start as a video coordinator with the Heat during their draft preparation.[111] This was a temporary job where he analyzed the game film of the college players and relayed information to the coaches. They were so impressed with his work ethic and ability to dissect these recordings, they offered him a job in that same role but full-time.

Once an official part of the Heat organization, Spoelstra continued to impress those around him with his ability to break down the game. It wasn't long before this video coordinator caught the attention of Coach Riley, one of the most well-respected coaches in the history of the NBA. He saw potential in this young man who went beyond analyzing game film and promoted him to assistant coach without any previous coaching or NBA-playing experience. While contributing to the Heat's success, he learned directly from Coach Riley how to inspire and motivate players to collectively work through challenges.[112]

In 2008, Coach Riley stepped down from his position to become president of operations for the team, culminating a 24-year coaching career that included five championships, three-time NBA Coach of the Year awards, and being the coach of the NBA all-star team nine times. In his new position as the Miami Heat president of operations, one of Pat Riley's first moves was to name Erik Spoelstra as the new head coach, who made his impact felt right away. Spoelstra took a team that had a record of 15-67 the previous year to the playoffs in his first season at the helm.[111]

Two seasons into his career, he received the greatest blessing and challenge a coach could receive: the acquisition of Lebron James and Chris Bosh, two of the most talented basketball players in the world at the time, to pair with their star Dwayne Wade. While any coach would love to have players of that caliber, it placed Coach Spoelstra in the unenviable position where he would have to win an NBA championship or be seen as a failure. This pressure could derail any team that did not have prepared leadership.

It almost proved too much in the 2013 NBA Finals when Coach Spoelstra faced with one the toughest situations of his coaching career. The Heat had just suffered one of the largest blowouts in NBA Finals history to fall behind the San Antonio Spurs 2-1 in a best of seven series. The Spurs were led by future Hall of Famers like Tim Duncan, Manu Ginobili, and Tony Parker, and Coach Spoelstra could not see a way to fight back against their efficient offensive attack.

Coach Spoelstra was at his lowest when he received a surprising visitor, his old commander Pat Riley. He provided his protégé with advice in his hour of need. Working together that night, they adjusted the Heat's plan to defeat the Spurs. When asked about his mentor's visit that night, Coach Spoelstra described it as "one of the most special moments of my professional career."[113]

After that championship win over San Antonio, Coach Spoelstra went on to win another NBA championship as well NBA Coach of the Year. Because Pat Riley took the opportunity to get to know those within his organization, he recognized Erik Spoelstra's talent and turned him into one of the top coaches in the NBA. It's easy for a leader to develop tunnel-vision and to perceive their people as assets to completing the mission, nothing more. Leaders who take the time to connect with others in their department can unlock hidden potential that could assist the company's success.

Maintain Healthy Boundaries

As leaders get to know their people, their relationships tend to transition from formal to more relaxed. There's nothing wrong with that; it's even encouraged for leaders to establish a good rapport with their team. Although something leaders need to be mindful of is not to let their relationships get to the point where it can comprise their job. When supervisors become too close to those they lead, it can affect the team dynamics and decisions they make for the benefit of their organizations. Create a fun, productive workplace while still remembering you are their boss, not their buddy.

"I Want People to Be Afraid of How Much They Love Me."

The American adaptation of the mockumentary TV show *The Office* (2005-2013) depicts the everyday lives of employees in the Scranton branch of small paper company Dunder Mifflin. Michael Scott, the regional manager, is an over-enthusiastic boss who constantly tries to win the approval of his employees. Unfortunately, he has difficulty distinguishing the line between professional and inappropriate, which prevents him from understanding individual boundaries. Michael stumbles from one awkward encounter to the next.

An example of Michael's disregard for the boundaries of his employees is when he has the company's IT technician set up email surveillance capabilities on his computer for the entire office. He wants to use this newfound power to search his staff's emails to find out what they are saying about him to their friends and among each other. What Michael discovers is that one of his employees is planning a party at their house and has invited everyone in the office – aside from Michael.

MISSION FIRST, PEOPLE ALWAYS

The rest of the day consists of Michael using not-so-subtle hints to pressure his employees for an invite. He asks each person about their weekend plans, but no one mentions the event. Having failed at guilting his employees, Michael adopts a bolder strategy: showing up to the party and acting like he is invited. Upon his arrival at the soiree, the mood understandably shifts. Although unsurprised by his sudden appearance, the party-goers remain uncomfortable.

Michael's main difficulty in dealing with his employees is that he has a compulsion to be liked personally by those that work for him. During an interview with the documentary crew, he shares his ideal relationship with his people: "Would I rather be feared or loved? Easy. Both. I want people to be afraid of how much they love me."[114] Although he means well, Michael's desire compromises his ability to effectively run his branch. His employees view him as an inconvenience they have to deal with as opposed to a valuable resource.

For a leader to accomplish anything of substance with their organization, they must maintain positive control. This means their instructions will be followed by their team no matter the difficulty or complexity of the situation. To ensure this is the case, a leader must separate themselves to a certain extent from their people; again, they must be the boss and not a friend. This can be uncomfortable to do, but the workplace will be better for everyone if the leader can stick to this mentality.

Drawing a Line

SMSgt. Burger was my flight chief during my first assignment in the Air Force, which was as the fabrication flight commander. In the military, it falls on SNCOs like SMSgt. Burger to assist in the development of young officers and show them how to lead airmen. In the beginning of my career, I frequently conversed with SMSgt. Burger on how to work through challenging leadership decisions and leaned heavily on his experience helped me navigate them effectively. He shared with me the instance in which he learned how to draw the line between being a leader and being a friend.

SMSgt. Burger recalled the difficulty he faced in being promoted from TSgt to MSgt. At first glance, a promotion might seem like an odd thing to struggle with, but a MSgt is the rank when enlisted officers go from NCO to SNCO. As the latter, enlisted maintainers transition from working on the aircraft to a more administrative role; they, along with officers, are responsible for the health, morale, performance, and discipline of all the maintainers in their unit. This promotion meant there was now a barrier between him and all the men he had worked with on the flight line for years.

His friends tried to take advantage of their relationship with him by pressuring him to give out the best shift assignments, letting some of the standards slide, and generally getting special treatment. MSgt. Burger made an important choice for himself going forward. At work, he had to be a boss, not a buddy. He made this clear in no uncertain terms to his friends that they would be treated the same as everyone else. That decision changed the nature of their relationship because, while they still enjoyed spending time together outside of work, he was no longer "one of the guys." Necessary boundaries of what was expected of his friends as their new leader had been established. This allowed MSgt. Burger to effectively lead all his people instead of catering to the few.

Leaders, like anyone else, want to be included in activities and liked among their staff. It's comfortable to be part of the group, but if those in leadership roles do not maintain professional boundaries, they will lose positive control of their organization. Finding the balance between getting to know the individuals you lead and becoming too familiar can be tough to determine at first; however, if you seek help from your own mentors and create clear parameters in the workplace, you will be okay. Being respected as a leader must come before being a pal. The clearer a leader is about these boundaries, the fewer problems there will be.

Get to Know Your People Reflection Questions

- What conscious efforts have you made to get to know your people as individuals inside and out of their work at your organization?
- Have these efforts helped you build relationships and trust with your people?
- If not, what do you think you could do more?

Find Out What Matters to Your People

- Do you know what your people care about outside of work?
- Do you know what concerns people in your organization are dealing with both professionally and personally?
- When you interact with your people, what is your ratio of talking to listening?

Build Your People Through Mentoring

- Brainstorm several qualities that make a good mentor in your opinion.
- Who are a few specific people in your organization who have potential that could be realized with your mentorship?
- Are you currently mentoring them or anyone else? If not, why?

Maintain Healthy Boundaries

- What actions between leaders and those they lead do you find inappropriate?
- If you carried out any of those actions, how would it degrade your ability to lead?

10

SERVE YOUR PEOPLE

My first leadership position in an AMU was serving as an assistant OIC under Capt. Channing. I had just come from serving as a flight commander of a back shop where I had cut my teeth as a maintenance officer, but had not faced some of the added pressures that came with an AMU job. When I reported the status of my airmen's maintenance in my prior role, I briefed it to our squadron's maintenance operations officer (MOO) – who was usually a major or captain – and they relayed it to the group commander, who would provide feedback to the MOO and back down to me. The process of dispatching information for the AMU meant briefing the aircraft status directly to the group commander. For a young lieutenant, the idea of briefing a colonel with decades of experience was nerve-racking.

If we were behind schedule on the maintenance of any aircraft, we had to describe in detail what repair decisions we made and why. There was little room for error and absolutely no tolerance for being unprepared to answer questions.

Whoever was supposed to brief the group commander every morning would take the hour before the brief to go over their notes and track down any information they still needed. As the newest member of this AMU's leadership team, I wouldn't be put in front of the group commander until Capt. Channing and the chief thought I was ready. After several days in my new role, Capt. Channing called me to her office before the routine meeting to practice delivering this data as if she were the group commander. She questioned me occasionally to make sure I comprehended what I was talking about. At the end of our first mock briefing, I was shocked by Capt. Channing's willingness to spend time helping me prepare when she could – and probably should – have organized her own documents for the presentation. She knew teaching me was a top priority as a leader, whose ultimate job was to serve their people. This exercise went on nearly every day for three weeks until we both felt I was ready to present.

The group commander seemed surprised when he saw me at the table, and he gave Capt. Channing a quizzical look that asked, "Are you sure he's ready to be here?" What he was not aware of was the amount of effort she had taken to make sure I was prepared and progressing as an officer.

Leaders are responsible for the performance and the wellbeing of all those within their organizations. Those committed to becoming a two-part leader must understand this and determine how they can use their position to serve the needs of their people. This will not only help their team perform at a higher level but build loyalty and mutual trust.

Do Not Use Your Position to Obtain Special Privileges

Leadership is a position of power, but this power is not meant to benefit that individual personally; rather, it provides them the opportunity to assist and support the people they oversee. Those who obtain leadership roles are individuals capable of guiding others in their organization toward success. This means supervisors are attentive to their department's needs and focused on working collaboratively instead of using their title to gain perks at the office. It is necessary for those who recently transitioned into leadership to remember they're still part of a team.

"I Just Knew It Wasn't the Right Thing to Do."

John McCain is most well-known for being a U.S. Senator from 1987-2018 and for running in the 2008 presidential election against Barack Obama. However, John McCain first made his name during the Vietnam War where, as a lieutenant commander (LCDR), he was held as a prisoner of war for over five years in a prison camp referred to as the "Hanoi Hilton." In 1967, LCDR McCain was captured after being shot down during his 23rd flying mission, which was an air attack of Hanoi's thermal power plant. During his crash and capture by the Vietnamese, LCDR McCain sustained severe injuries; both arms and one of his knees were broken and he received stabs to the groin and ankle by his captors on the way to the prison camp.

Living conditions at the "Hanoi Hilton" were some of the harshest for any of the POWs during the Vietnam War. LCDR McCain was not treated for any of his injuries and was routinely waken randomly – day or night – to be tortured. He and others were malnourished to the point where he had lost over 50 pounds six weeks into his imprisonment.[115] On top of that, he spent most of the first two years there in solitary confinement.

Things took a surprising turn for LCDR McCain in 1968 when his captors realized he was the son of Admiral McCain, the newly-appointed commander of the U.S. Forces in the Pacific. The prison camps' commander visited the American soldier personally and offered him early release to his country. LCDR McCain drew back on his training as a military officer, which stated that he was not permitted to accept special favors from the enemy.[116] He knew that there were prisoners at the camp who had been serving far longer than him; he considered his freedom a privilege based on his father's military position. With this in mind, McCain made the decision to stay behind with the other POWs in Hanoi. Insulted by his defiance, the commander reportedly told him: "Now it will be very bad for you, Mac Kane." The U.S. pilot's torture and mistreatment continued until his release in 1973.[113]

Regardless of the hunger and pain he underwent, LCDR McCain understood that his and his father's position in the military did not entitle him to favorable treatment. In fact, because of his career, he held himself to a higher standard. Upon looking back at why he refused to go home, LCDR McCain said, "I just knew it wasn't the right thing to do. I knew they wouldn't have offered it to me if I hadn't been the son of an admiral."[117] Leaders who do not take advantage of the power they have to benefit themselves win the respect and the trust of those they lead. With that respect, they motivate and guide their team to greater heights.

But it can be easy for some people in leadership to feel they are *entitled* to special treatment. With all the extra responsibility they carry, they think they should be able to reap all the benefits their position can afford them. Once this kind of behavior and attitude begin, a leader will zero in on what they can obtain individually as opposed to what benefits they can provide for their people. Those with ulterior motives for personal gain will not be effective as a supervisor for long.

"Be Prepared!"

The Lion King is one of Disney's classic animated films, which depicts the story of Simba, a lion cub growing up in the heart of the Pride Lands. In this tale, King Mufasa's brother Scar shows obvious disdain for him and Simba and for the power they hold; Scar feels he is more deserving of the title due to his intelligence versus Mufasa, who he assumes only became king because of his brute strength.

While Mufasa teaches Simba about how to be a king and protect the Pride Lands, Scar schemes how to take Mufasa's place as ruler. He enlists the help of the hyenas – vicious scavengers that have been banned from the Pride Lands – to put his plans into motion. One day, Scar leads Simba into a canyon gorge, promising that his father will meet him there as a surprise. Simba waits alone while Scar signals for the hyenas to trigger a wildebeest stampede, putting the lion cub right in their crosshairs.

Upon hearing his son is in danger, Mufasa rushes to the gorge and saves Simba. Scar watches this play out from above, waiting to make his move. Just when it seems

MISSION FIRST, PEOPLE ALWAYS

Mufasa has, against all odds, secured a happy ending for both himself and Simba, Scar shoves his brother off a cliff.

After killing Mufasa, Scar orders his hyenas to kill Simba who escapes through thorn thickets. With the death of Mufasa and the disappearance of Simba, Scar completes his plot to become king.

Once Scar gains power, he reintroduces hyenas into the Pride Lands. This immediately makes Scar's subjects – the lionesses – second-class citizens by forcing them to hunt continuously to satisfy Scar and the hyenas' appetites. This practice of overhunting destroys the balance of life within their area, causing herds to move on to better feeding grounds. The Pride Lands becomes a barren wasteland under Scar's leadership.

The lionesses confront Scar and, instead of taking responsibility and finding solutions to help save his subjects, Scar blames the direness of their situation on *their* lack of effort. This becomes clear during an argument[118] between Scar and Sarabi, the head lioness:

Scar: Where is your hunting party? They are not doing their job.

Sarabi: Scar, there is no food. The herds have moved on.

Scar: No, you're just not looking hard enough!

Sarabi: It's over. There is nothing left. We have only one choice. We must leave Pride Rock.

Scar: We are not going anywhere!

Sarabi: Then you have sentenced us to death!

Scar: Then so be it.

Sarabi: You can't do that!

Scar: I'm the king! I can do whatever I want!

Serve Your People

Sarabi: If you were half the king Mufasa was...

Scar: (strikes Sarabi to the ground) I'm ten times the king Mufasa was!

Scar is enraged; he cannot grasp how Mufasa successfully ruled the Pride Lands while he flounders. What he doesn't understand is that he was destined for failure before ever becoming king because he wanted the power only to serve himself. This selfish style of leadership will never motivate people to perform their best work. Leaders who realize their position does not entitle them to more perks can win the hearts and minds of their people.

Remember the Purpose of Your Authority

By virtue of their position, leaders are afforded more power than others. It is an extension of trust from those who make up an organization, for they rely on their leaders to use their status to make beneficial decisions for everyone. Leaders have a responsibility to consistently check their actions to ensure what they are doing is altruistic versus selfish. The temptation to misuse their title is a challenge many people have succumbed to, derailing otherwise successful potential.

The Watergate Scandal

Most remember President Richard Nixon for resigning in disgrace as he faced an almost-certain impeachment. What is less memorable is that, before the scandal that torpedoed his career, President Nixon was on track to become one of the most successful and popular presidents in modern U.S. history. After winning a close election in 1968 over Vice President Hubert Humphrey, President Nixon and his administration entered office with little fanfare or expectations. Many observers expected him to be a "do nothing" president, merely keeping the status quo.

Despite those low standards, the Nixon administration hit the ground running. President Nixon undertook numerous important reforms in welfare policy, civil rights, and law enforcement. He was also strong on environmental issues, proposing the legislation that created the Occupational Safety and Health Administration (OSHA) and the Environmental Protection Agency (EPA).[119] Beyond that, many view the most important achievement of President Nixon's career as his establishment of direct relations with the People's Republic of China. In February of 1972, President Nixon became the first American president to ever visit China while in office. This event not only improved our global connections as a growing world power, but gave the U.S. more leverage in dealings with the Soviet Union.

When the 1972 election came, the Democrats nominated Senator George McGovern from South Dakota, who ran on a platform of bringing the Vietnam War to an immediate end and establishing a minimum wage.[120] Despite this, he struggled against Nixon's strong economy and foreign policy success. Americans viewed President Nixon as a strong and capable leader, someone they could trust to make the right decision. Going into the election, Democrats were not optimistic about their candidate's chances again the incumbent, but nothing could have prepared them for the outcome. Nixon received a majority of the vote in 49 of the 50 states, including McGovern's home state.[121] This was one of the most lopsided victories in any American presidential election and signaled the American people were unified in a way that they had not been in years.

Not long after this triumph, Nixon's political career was flung into disarray. Allegations surfaced against the Nixon administration of breaking into the offices of Senator McGovern and planting surveillance equipment during the election. These reports, which started as a minor annoyance, quickly became a major issue that led to the appointment of a special prosecutor to investigate the accusations and how far the conspiracy went.

Serve Your People

After months of shocking updates as new revelations unfolded, the ultimate news finally came out: President Nixon had abused his power and was fully aware of the "Watergate Scandal." He had utilized all of his presidential powers to cover up these crimes; Nixon was forced to either resign or be impeached. On August 9, 1974, Richard Nixon became the first president in American history to resign from office, forever fracturing the trust between the American people and the federal government.[122] We do not remember all that Nixon accomplished in his career, only how far he fell.

For leaders to be successful, they must realize how their actions matter within their organization. An abuse of power tells others that they are no longer looking out for their best interests, which creates tension in the workplace. If a manager believes they can wield their powers however they wish because of their accomplishments, they won't see these actions as offensive; they might even feel protected from potential consequences. That again damages the relationship they have with their team. Individuals in leadership roles have to remember their power comes *from* the people and is meant to serve the many instead of the few.

Give People the Tools They Need to Succeed

A leader serving their people effectively does not require them to coddle or to perform every task for their staff. It can be as simple as getting their people the tools they need to succeed. Often, those in leadership have access to materials, knowledge, or privileges that are essential to daily activities. With those resources, team members will be freed from any superficial barriers that stand in the way of efficient work, such as asking the higher-ups to obtain necessary office supplies or new software.

MISSION FIRST, PEOPLE ALWAYS

Turning Students into Leaders

  The movie *October Sky* – based on *Rocket Boys* – details the formative teenage years of Homer Hickam, a NASA aerospace engineer who designed spacecraft and trained crews for space travel. He grows up in the small West Virginian town Coalwood, where he sees two options for his future: join the military or work in the coal mine like his father. This all changes for Homer in 1957 however, when the Russian government launches Sputnik into space. This historic event sparks the boy's interest in space travel, rockets, and a life outside of Coalwood.

  As Homer dives further into the world of spacecraft, he enlists the help of his friends at Big Creek High School to form the Big Creek Missile Agency (BCMA). The BCMA attempts to model rockets and missiles with little success; the closer they get to a successful launch, the more often it blows through the fence in Homer's backyard. They continue making improvements, but did not know how to prevail.

  One day, their chemistry teacher, Miss Freida Riley, shows the boys how to create a more stable form of rocket fuel through simple chemical reactions. Just like Homer, Miss Riley understands there are limited educational opportunities for the kids she taught at Big Creek; she plays an important role in nourishing the academic curiosity of the students, specifically those in the BCMA. As they progress in their journey, Miss Riley supports their learning and encourages them to venture beyond.

  When they reach the limit to what they can do on their own, Miss Riley finds a book on rocket science for them to study. Handing Homer the book, she says, "All I've done is give you a book. You have to have the courage to learn what's inside it."[123]

  Although Miss Riley knows she cannot learn the material for them, she provides them with the opportunities and resources to succeed. When the BCMA wants to start Big Creek's first calculus class, it is Miss Riley who campaigns to the principal to help make it happen. She uses her role as an educator to arrange avenues for these students to improve themselves and exceed their comfort zones. It is also Miss Riley who continually pressures the BCMA to enter their work on rockets into the national science fair, which they eventually win. This victory sets the BCMA on a path to attend college, an unheard-of feat for children in Coalwood, WV in the 1950s.

Miss Riley knew her prosperity as a leader depended on the success of those she taught, which is why she supported the BCMA. She used her influence as a teacher to give her students opportunities that could fulfill their greatest potential. In 2005, Miss Riley was entered in the honorary registry for the National Museum of Education; in her entry, it reads, "It was her encouragement that brought these boys into manhood as believers in knowledge and hard-work."[123]

When a leader provides their people with the tools they need to excel, they are repaid by that ensuing success. Innovation inspires those in an organization to work for the joy of it instead of just running out the clock. People who feel supported by their leadership team will be more willing to contribute.

Ford's Most Valuable Asset

Henry Ford, founder of Ford Motor Company, was a man whose vision was ahead of his time. He is remembered as an important figure who modernized the automotive industry as well manufacturing processes. Where Mr. Ford truly showed his vision as a leader was how he treated those within his organization. He brought about changes no one understood at the time, but that would cement his company as a force to be reckoned with for the next 100-plus years.

In the early 1900s, America underwent the Industrial Revolution, and manufacturing technology entered every industry at an alarming rate. These corporations set up their businesses in urban areas, where plenty of unskilled labor could be found. Wage laborers in this era made $2.40 a day, which is about the same as $62 in today's currency.[124] These low wages placed many

Americans in a downward spiral of poverty that they had little hope of escaping.

Mr. Ford made changes within his company that shocked the rest of the business world. In 1914, he more than doubled the pay of his employees by changing the minimum wage to $5.00. This allowed his employees to earn a reasonable living wage. Such an increase in pay was an investment in his people; it was a way to improve his organization. He said, "If the floor sweeper's heart is in his job, he can save us five dollars a day by picking up small tools instead of sweeping them out."[125]

Twelve years later, Mr. Ford shortened the work week for his employees to five days. Ford Motor Company was the first major U.S. company to instill this type of schedule, which is now common practice all over the world. On top of giving his staff Saturdays and Sundays off, he limited their daily shifts to eight hours as opposed to the industry norm of 10 or 15 hours.[123] Mr. Ford saw his employees as valuable cogs in his machine and treated them accordingly. Mr. Ford's son Edsel expounded on the value the company placed on their people:

> Every man needs more than one day a week for rest and recreation… The Ford Company always has sought to promote [an] ideal home life for its employees. We believe that in order to live properly, every man should have more time to spend with his family.[126]

After making these adjustments, many thought Ford would lose its place at the top of the automotive industry. But the following year's records depicted the opposite; the increased pay of his employees and the corporation's sales shot up nearly 20%. By 1920, Ford Motor Company's profits had more than tripled, selling more than 1 million cars a year.[121] As one of the highest performing businesses in the country, Ford became a shining example how the rest of the U.S. could treat their people well, provide all of the necessary resources, and still be successful. Today, the idea of paying employees a living wage and giving people sufficient time off to have a life outside of work is accepted as a best practice.

Leaders first should anticipate or listen to the needs of those they oversee. Once they understand, they must go beyond making their team feel heard and produce the materials that were requested. Employees want to work hard to repay their supervisors who help them succeed because they feel important to the company's bigger picture.

Servant Leadership Will Build Internal Motivation

In any industry, those within an organization are motivated by various factors. The first one that comes to mind is compensation. Some leaders think that, in order to convince their people to work harder, all they have to give them is more money, equity, PTO days, or similar perks. As studies and my experience have shown, compensation only motivates people so far. Internal ambition to produce more for the company depends on other variables like autonomy, ability to master their craft, and how people feel they are treated by higher-ups. This is why practicing servant leadership – the idea that a leader's role is to serve their people and help their development – is so important.

The Inverted Pyramid

Southwest Airlines, founded in 1967, is a commercial airline company based out of Dallas. It is well-known for low prices, amazing customer service, and being a great place to work. Every year for the last decade, Southwest Airlines has made Glassdoor's list of ten best companies to work for in the U.S.[127] This success goes back to the idea of servant leadership, which inspires their employees from the head of the organization all the way down.[128]

Colleen Barrett, president emeritus of Southwest, explains how her organization implements this in a completive industry:

> Our pyramid is upside down from most companies. We clearly and proudly proclaim that our employees are our

MISSION FIRST, PEOPLE ALWAYS

first customer in terms of priority, our passengers are our second customer, and our shareholders are our third customer.[129]

Although this may sound counterintuitive to how businesses make money in today's profit-driven world, Mrs. Barrett delves deeper into this concept as she presents to students at the Wharton School of Management:

> At the top of our pyramid, in terms of the most important priority, we have our employees. 85% of my time is spent on [them] and on delivering proactive customer service to our employees. If I do a good enough job of that […] they in turn spend their life trying to assure that the second most important customers to us in our pyramid, which is our passenger, feels good about the service that they are getting.[130]

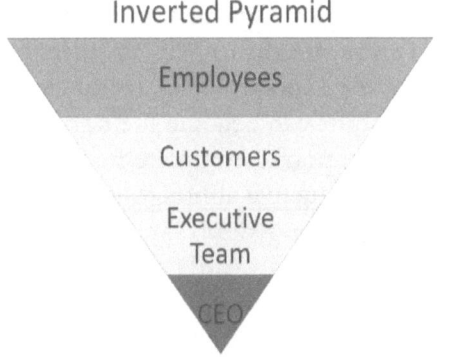

Southwest Airlines Management Priorities
Inverted Pyramid
Employees
Customers
Executive Team
CEO

Leadership at Southwest Airlines has not only turned this business model into a company that has one of the highest employee satisfaction rates in the world but a corporate success.[131] They have grown from the regional airline that only flew between Dallas, Houston, and San Antonio into a giant in the industry that flies to over 100 locations globally. During its climb, Southwest has also posted a profit every year for the past 35 years; even during the recession of 2008 that devastated other businesses, Southwest continued to grow.[130]

This company excels in an industry where many fail because their leadership understands one simple principle. If a leader takes care of their people, then their people will return the favor. Herb Kelleher, founder of Southwest Airlines, wanted to build a company where a culture of respect trickled down from employees to customers. When people are recognized as unique assets instead of tools, production and satisfaction skyrocket. It all starts with a leader valuing the wellbeing of their people.

The 10-Hour Rule

Another example of being attuned to employees' needs is how the Air Force aimed to prevent drawn-out shifts for those in AMUs. When facing the prospect of a maintenance death spiral, a common response for officers is to try to just work their way out of it. Maintainers throughout the Air Force are familiar with 12-plus-hour shifts that can go on for months to help stabilize their unit, so it operates at the expected level. If not carefully managed, these long shifts can become the norm – and a crutch that leaders lean upon to complete necessary tasks. This schedule can be productive although difficult in the short-term; however, if extended too far, it has the potential to completely drain an AMU of its morale.

During a maintenance group leadership meeting, our commander Col. Avery announced that all maintainers were limited to 10-hour shifts from then on. Our entire leadership was astonished by the news. The maintainers in our AMU normally only worked 10-hour shifts, but we found ourselves relying on longer days to avoid the maintenance death spiral. We mentioned our concerns about how to manage the flying schedule with these new restrictions. Col. Avery, however, did not budge; he challenged us as leaders to find ways to be more efficient instead of resorting to longer stints. He was adamant that the maintainers were not going to pay the price for any of their leadership's failing to run their organizations productively. This forced us to take a closer look at our current scheduling practices, manpower allotments, and even the long-term feasibility of our flying schedule.

Amazingly, this new policy not only pushed AMU leaders to improve, but urged the maintainers to become more adept. They were motivated by the commitment to their wellbeing that the maintenance group showed them and stepped up to the task. There was an increase in shorter breaks and less joking around while performing duties. Supervisors and maintainers on the flight line strived to get as much as possible done in their 10-hour shifts. Before long, some AMUs increased their production.

Col. Avery knew from the start what took us a while to learn – true leadership resides in taking care of your people. It is a concept that can be difficult for leaders to remember when there are so many pressures to meet set organization-wide objectives. Those who find operational success by applying that demand on their staff will find it short-lived. If leaders balance the workload and the attention to team members, they will build a culture of productivity, respect, and appreciation within an organization.

Measure Your Success by the Commitment of Your People

How can you tell if you're serving your team properly? There are no established indicators that show how those in leadership are meeting the needs of their people; yearly reviews don't even demonstrate honest feedback. Thus, the level of devotion and loyalty shown by those in the organization is a sign of successful servant leadership. For a supervisor to gain that kind of support, it signifies their staff trusts them to make decisions in their best interests.

"I Am Spartacus!"

The 1960 movie *Spartacus* follows a former slave turned gladiator who becomes the leader of a revolution against the slave masters in Rome. The protagonist, Spartacus, is introduced as a belligerent slave assigned to work in the mining pit. Luckily, he is noticed by a Roman businessman who is impressed with his ferocity and is purchased with the intention of having him train as a fighter. During this coaching, Spartacus earns the respect of his fellow slaves for depicting himself as a man of integrity even in the face of severe punishments from the slave masters.

The turning point for Spartacus comes when he is disarmed in the gladiator pit during a private match for wealthy spectators. Instead of killing the movie's protagonist, his opponent turns his weapons on the Roman audience. Inspired by this act of defiance as well as his own mistreatment, Spartacus leads the slaves and gladiators in a revolt, overthrowing the guards and captors. After the slaves free themselves, they elect Spartacus as their leader. He then promises to flee to Italy with them and return them to their homelands.

In their journey to vacate Rome and the injustice of slavery, their numbers swell as individuals flock to their cause. Under Spartacus, they successfully withstand Roman mercenaries ordered to terminate their rebellion. Spartacus resists alongside his people; his esteem and legend spreads across the country with each victory. Freedom is within reach when Spartacus's army is lured into a trap and defeated.

With Spartacus and his followers back in chains, the Romans present what seems like a generous offer. If the slaves deliver Spartacus, the captured individuals can go back to their masters unpunished. Spartacus is the only one the Romans want to suffer. It is made known to all the slaves that, when Spartacus is caught, he will die by crucifixion.

What follows this offer is one of the most iconic movie scenes in cinematic history. As Spartacus is about to give himself up to the Romans, the man to his right stands and shouts, "I am Spartacus!"[132] This is followed by a second, then a third; it continues until every man is on his feet. The Romans – equally amazed and outraged by this display – decide to kill all the men to ensure the death of Spartacus. The final scene depicts a road into Rome lined with crucified men.

There have been many stories told about leaders, both real and fictional, who have led soldiers into battles and rebellions. What makes Spartacus stand out as a great commander is not any grandiose accomplishment, but what his people were willing to do for him.

The Ultimate Sacrifice

In January 2018, hundreds of residents of North Ogden, UT filled the streets to see off Mayor Brent Taylor as he left for the Utah National Guard in Afghanistan. This, his fourth deployment for the National Guard major, would be his most difficult as he had to leave his wife and seven children for a year.[133] This may seem odd for constituents to be so involved in what would normally be an intimate family event, but for Mayor Taylor, it fell in line with who he was as a leader.

When Mayor Taylor informed his 19,000 residents about his deployment, he shared the message with them that this kind of "service is really what leadership is really all about." Such a display resonated with the townsfolk who knew Mayor Taylor from his eight-year tenure as mayor.

Judy Visoke was a constituent who voiced how many experienced Mayor Taylor's leadership:

> I don't politically align with him… But I noticed in his running of this town that he treated everyone with respect, and he listened, and he didn't bring his politics into the mix. He's just unlike any mayor I've ever experienced.[134]

When news broke that Major Taylor had been killed in action, his family, along with the people that he served, were heartbroken. Messages from the governor of Utah, the state's two senators, the president of Afghanistan, as well as hundreds of residents of North Ogden flooded in to comfort the family. Mayor Taylor's funeral was attended by over 1,000 mourners who came to offer their support, an unheard-of event in such a small community.[135] They didn't want to miss their opportunity to honor the memory of a leader they knew had made sacrifices for his town, his state, and his country.

Those in leadership often go through their careers without knowing the impact of their actions on their team members. The ability to motivate one's cohorts can be difficult to determine – especially in today's world where people are disconnected from each other by technology – but it *is* possible to measure. Followers react more positively in their duties and in reviews if they believe they have a strong leader. If you recognize your people acting when not required, that is dedication, and it means you have served properly.

Serve Your People Reflection Questions

- What privileges, if any, do you receive from your position within your organization?
- Are those privileges justified?
- Do they create a perceived lack of equality between you and your people?

Remember the Purpose of Your Authority

- In what ways have you seen past leaders abuse their power? How did that impact the way they were viewed within the organization?
- Have you ever abused your power as a leader? If so, how?

Give Your People the Tools to Succeed

- What are some challenges your people currently face in doing their jobs?
- How could you use your position to remove those obstacles?

Servant Leadership Will Build Internal Motivation

- How have you used your authority as a leader to serve your people specifically?
- What impact did those acts of service have on the people in your organization?

Measure Your Success by the Commitment of Your People

- Have you ever taken notice of how your people generally respond to your acts of service or giving back within the organization?
- If so, what responses and attitudes did you observe?

11

THE FINAL CHALLENGE

Lean on What You Know, Build What You Don't

  The fundamental principles in this book are important for every leader to know and use. If implemented correctly, these precepts have the power to help any new boss transform their organization's processes and assist their people in reaching their greatest potential. My only caution to any reader after completing this is not to be frustrated with yourself if you recognize that you lack mastery of the topics I've mentioned. Developing the skills of a two-part leader takes time and practice – and it will involve many failures along the way. But failures are just lessons.

  Most people, no matter how long they are in leadership, never develop themselves fully as both a manager and as a motivator. In lieu of self-improvement and conscious training, people often rely on their natural leadership traits, leaning more on either management *or* motivation. Even some who were considered history's greatest leaders had gaps in their leadership skillset.

  Jeff Bezos is the founder and former CEO of Amazon, one the most successful companies in modern history. In his time at the helm of Amazon, Mr. Bezos took the company from an online bookstore to streaming service, webservice provider, and one of the largest global retailers.[136][137] Mr. Bezos clearly has unmatched talent as a manager, leveraging his skill to create a technology giant.

MISSION FIRST, PEOPLE ALWAYS

While that is all true, the technology mogul's legacy becomes more complicated when the topic turns to how he treated those who worked for him. Amazon has focused its incredible efficiency on how to get the most out its employees, which is why the company monitors their movements and idle time, even tracking their steps during the day. Staff members have reported being fired for a single day of low productivity. According to sources from within Amazon, Mr. Bezos manages this way because he believes people are inherently lazy and letting them act without these restrictions would result in a "march toward mediocrity."[138] This extreme behavior reveals that, even though Mr. Bezos is one of the most successful businessmen in the U.S., he still has cracks in his leadership.

Another example of a great leader who failed to master every aspect of being a two-part leader was Abraham Lincoln. Although he served as U.S. president more than 100 years ago, he is still universally recognized as one of the greatest political leaders in American history. President Lincoln led the country through the Civil War. Even more impressive than leading the Union to victory was his ability to reunite the country after the war. He demonstrated courage to stand firm against enemies and empathetically reached out to those opponents after their defeat.

Despite his success as a leader, he also had failures that resulted directly from a lack of effective management. In 1834, Lincoln opened a general store in New Salem, IL and, less than a year later, his business went bankrupt. The debt of that business followed him for over 17 years.[139] He also used his power as a leader of the majority party in the state's legislature to push an array of ambitious infrastructure bills that committed millions of taxpayer dollars to widening rivers, building railroads, digging canals, and creating roads. Although Lincoln's intent was to design a thriving economy's foundation, these projects were never finished and resulted in debt that crippled Illinois for years afterward.[109]

Even those who are universally recognized for their leadership like Bezos or Lincoln experience shortcomings. There are very few people who have the innate instincts necessary to make them a complete two-part leader without training. We all possess strengths that come to us naturally, but there will always be important principles that seem completely foreign and uncomfortable to us. The key is to lean on what comes easily while developing what is difficult.

A person who is a natural motivator – an individual to whom others flock – must also practice the principles of effective management. They need to delegate and follow up, to manage their time, and to communicate clearly. The same goes for a person who is a natural manager; they need to get to know and serve their staff members on a deeper level. They must push themselves to inspire those around them to become more than a manager – to become a two-part leader.

What Kind of Leader Will You Be?

The next step is for you to decide what kind of leader you want to become, which involves more than just determining if you can lead your people, but *how* you want to do so. This requires you to look beyond the leadership skills we have gone over in this book and seek the answer within yourself. It will be a decision based on your personal beliefs and values. How can you best translate those into the workplace?

One of my OICs approached me while I was working in an AMU and gave me what at the time seemed like a very odd assignment. She wanted me to create a leadership credo – or a statement of beliefs – that would guide my actions as a leader. I'd never heard of anything like this and was cynical at first, thinking of it as a trivial exercise. Capt. Channing insisted I give it serious time and consideration. She ensured me that, if done right, it would serve as a compass in my career, keeping me set on the path I wanted to go.

It forced me to look beyond who I was in my leadership position at the time and think about who I wanted to be going forward. In doing that, I reflected on leaders I had read about, observed, or even served under and pulled pieces of what I admired most. Some of those individuals who influenced the leader I wanted to be are in this book. I also considered how my personal beliefs I held dear – including service, humility, fairness, and my faith in God – factored into how I would make decisions.

These efforts to forge my leadership style did not result in a cohesive narrative, but separate points that, when viewed together, sculpted a rough sketch that I could fill out as time went by. This gave me the power to pivot when needed. At least I had an image in my mind that I worked toward as I continued to gain experience.

My challenge to any reader is to consciously choose what values and beliefs form your leadership style. These are important to consider even while building your foundation in a new position of power and the skillset needed to succeed in it. You don't have to design a leadership credo, but you should be intentional with what precepts you lead by. Look to those you admire or, better yet, evaluate those whose leadership you find abhorrent and why. Learn from these individuals; let them help you become the leader your people deserve. As you move forward in your chosen career, these principles coupled with the concentrated effort of developing your two-part leadership, will allow you improve the performance of your organization along with the lives of those who work in it.

My Leadership Credo

- Respect is not a privilege that is earned. It is a right given to everyone up and down the chain of command.

- Seek to understand and then to be understood.

- Be flexible when you can; stand firm when you must.

- Whatever standards are in place apply to everyone; rank does not change standards.

- No matter how good your processes or people are, the success of the mission is based on communication.

- Be a situational leader. Do not draw lines in the sand.

- Never be afraid to say you don't know. Make sure to find answers quickly.

- Come to meetings prepared with something of value to ask or say.

- If you are early, then you are on time. If you are on time, you are late.

- Authority is given through rank; influence is earned through effective leadership.

- My priorities in life are my family, then my faith, and finally my career. I will make decisions in life based on those priorities.

APPENDIX

Air Force Maintenance Organizational Structure

* The **MXG** is the group responsible for all aircraft and support equipment maintenance performs on base.
* **AMXS** is the squadron responsible for all aircraft flying hours and maintenance.
* **CMS** & **EMS** are made up of back shops or flights that specialize in specific areas of aircraft maintenance.
* **AMUs** are where aircraft are housed and maintained. AMUs perform all general aircraft maintenance and servicing.

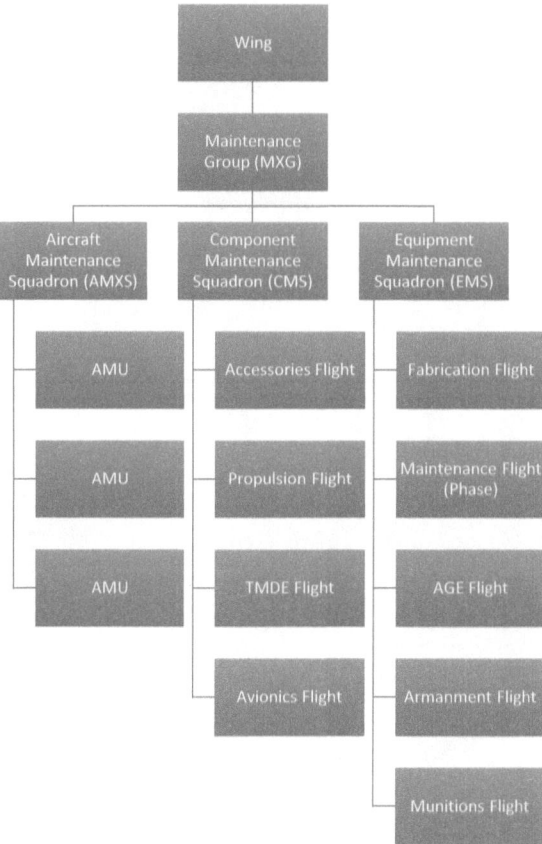

Air Force Rank Hierarchy

Enlisted

Airman Basic	AB	E-1
Airman	Amn	E-2
Airman First Class	A1C	E-3
Senior Airman	SrA	E-4
Staff Sergeant	SSgt	E-5
Technical Sergeant	TSgt	E-6
Master Sergeant	MSgt	E-7
Senior Master Sergeant	SMSgt	E-8
Chief Master Sergeant	CMSgt	E-9

Officers

Second Lieutenant	2Lt	O-1
First Lieutenant	1Lt	O-2
Captain	Capt	O-3
Major	Maj	O-4
Lieutenant Colonel	Lt Col	O-5
Colonel	Col	O-6
Brigadier General	Brig Gen	O-7
Major General	Maj Gen	O-8
Lieutenant General	Lt Gen	O-9
General	Gen	O-10

NOTES

[1] Velasquez, Robert. "13 Shocking Leadership Development Statistics." Infopro Learning. July 13, 2020. https://www.infoprolearning.com/infographic/13-shocking-leadership-development-statistics-infopro-learning/.

[2] Hamm, Robert. "Mission First, People Always." U.S. Air Force, July 15, 2005. https://www.af.mil/News/Commentaries/Display/Article/142195/mission-first-people-always/.

[3] *Spider-Man*. Sony Pictures, 2002.

[4] "Civil War Casualties." *American Battlefield Trust*. April 29, 2021. www.battlefields.org/learn/articles/civil-war-casualties?gclid=Cj0KCQjw5uWGBhCTARIsAL70sLKHpc0l69slojgiz6yRTr39J7rCHeXL8xBBY8O3DdB-_uXQ4pYbGBcaAgxPEALw_wcB.

[5] "Battle of Gettysburg." *History.com*. A&E Television Networks, October 29, 2009. https://www.history.com/topics/american-civil-war/battle-of-gettysburg.

[6] Lincoln, Abraham. "Lincoln's Unsent Letter to George Meade." American Battlefield Trust. Accessed April 10, 2020. https://www.battlefields.org/learn/primary-sources/lincolns-unsent-letter-george-meade.

[7] Teitel, Amy Shira. "The Time NASA Lost a Mars Orbiter Because of a Metric System Mix-up." Motherboard. Vice,

September 11, 2014. https://motherboard.vice.com/en_us/article/qkvzb5/the-time-nasa-lost-a-mars-orbiter-because-of-a-metric-system-mixup.

[8] "NASA Finally Goes Metric." Space.com, January 8, 2007. https://www.space.com/3332-nasa-finally-metric.html.

[9] "System Failures Case Studies – Lost in Translation." *National Aeronautics and Space Administration* 3, no. 5 (August 2009): 1–4.

[10] *Coach Carter*. California: Paramount, 2005.

[11] Spitzer, Justin, and Owen Ellickson. "Labor." *Superstore* 1, no. 11. NBC, February 22, 2016.

[12] Spitzer, Justin, and Jackie Clarke. "Strike." *Superstore*, 2, no. 1. NBC, September 22, 2016.

[13] "Martin Luther King, Jr." History.com. A&E Television Networks, November 9, 2009. http://www.history.com/topics/black-history/martin-luther-king-jr.

[14] "'I Have a Dream' Speech." History.com. A&E Television Networks, November 30, 2017. https://www.history.com/topics/civil-rights-movement/i-have-a-dream-speech.

[15] Johnson, Ben. "The Evacuation of Dunkirk." Historic UK, April 30, 2020. https://www.historic-uk.com/HistoryUK/HistoryofBritain/Evacuation-of-Dunkirk/.

[16] "We Shall Fight on the Beaches." International Churchill Society. Curtis Brown, April 13, 2017.

https://winstonchurchill.org/resources/speeches/1940-the-finest-hour/we-shall-fight-on-the-beaches/.

[17] *Forever Strong.* Crane Movie Co., 2008.

[18] Smith, Brian T. "High School Rugby: Larry Gelwix, Highland Capture 20th National Title." The Salt Lake Tribune, March 21, 2011. http://archive.sltrib.com/article.php?id=51859968&itype=CMSID.

[19] Card, Orson. *Ender's Game.* New York: Tor Books. 1985.

[20] Manas, Jerry. *Napoleon on Project Management: Timeless Lessons in Planning, Execution, and Leadership.* Nashville: HarperCollins Leadership, 2008.

[21] Hurwitz, Mitchell and John Levenstein. "Top Banana." *Arrested Development* 1, no. 2. Fox, November 2, 2003.

[22] Byers, J. Harold. "The Miracle Mind of Nikola Tesla from the Tesla Universe Article Collection." Tesla Universe, November 24, 2019. https://teslauniverse.com/nikola-tesla/articles/miracle-mind-nikola-tesla.

[23] Falksen, GD. "The Tesla Tragedy." Tor.com, November 1, 2010. https://www.tor.com/2010/11/01/the-tesla-tragedy/.

[24] "Genghis Khan." History.com. A&E Television Networks, November 9, 2009. https://www.history.com/topics/china/genghis-khan.

[25] Rogers, Abby. "The 10 Greatest Empires in The History of The World." *Business Insider,* November 9, 2011. https://www.businessinsider.com/the-10-greatest-empires-in-history-2011-9.

[26] Axson, Scooby. "Ricky Williams Says Bad Quarterback Play Led to His Decision to Retire from the NFL in 2004." *Sports Illustrated*. Sports Illustrated, October 30, 2014. https://www.si.com/nfl/2014/10/30/ricky-dolphins-ricky-williams-retirement-bad-quarterbacks.

[27] "DI Men's Lacrosse Championship History." NCAA.com, June 17, 2021. www.ncaa.com/history/lacrosse-men/d1.

[28] Luther, Hal. "SU Lacrosse: How They Won It." Training & Conditioning, January 29, 2015. https://training-conditioning.com/news/su-lacrosse-how-they-won-it/.

[29] "How Syracuse Lacrosse Builds Speed Endurance." Stack.com, September 1, 2009. http://www.stack.com/a/how-syracuse-lacrosse-builds-speed-endurance.

[30] *Ocean's Eleven*. Warner Brothers, 2001.

[31] *Iron Man*. Paramount, 2008.

[32] Oaks, Dallin H. "Desire." The Church of Jesus Christ of Latter-Day Saints, May 2011. www.churchofjesuschrist.org/study/liahona/2011/05/saturday-afternoon-session/desire?lang=eng.

[33] Gold, Matea. "Salt Lake Olympics Were Romney's Golden Moment." Los Angeles Times, July 27, 2012. http://articles.latimes.com/2012/jul/27/nation/la-na-romney-olympics-20120727-1.

[34] Whitmer, Caleb. "Romney, Leadership, and the 2002 Olympics." National Review, September 3, 2012. https://www.nationalreview.com/corner/romney-leadership-and-2002-olympics-caleb-whitmer/.

[35] Adebowale, Temi. "The Design Flaw That Caused the 1986 Challenger Disaster." MSN News, September 16, 2020. www.msn.com/en-us/news/technology/the-design-flaw-that-caused-the-1986-challenger-disaster/ar-BB1975CG.

[36] Berkes, Howard. "Challenger Engineer Who Warned of Shuttle Disaster Dies." NPR, March 21, 2016. https://www.npr.org/sections/thetwo-way/2016/03/21/470870426/challenger-engineer-who-warned-of-shuttle-disaster-dies.

[37] Denning, Steve. "Nelson Mandela: A Leader Who Listened." *Forbes*. Forbes Magazine, December 8, 2013. https://www.forbes.com/sites/stevedenning/2013/12/08/nelson-mandela-a-leader-who-listened/#5a36a9d375ba.

[38] Stern, Joshua Michael, Mark Hulme, and Matt Whiteley. *Jobs*. United States: Open Road Films, 2013.

[39] Martyris, Nina. "The Most Punctual Man in India." *Lapham's Quarterly*, December 2, 2014. https://www.laphamsquarterly.org/roundtable/most-punctual-man-india.

[40] Oaks, Dallin H. "Good, Better, Best." The Church of Jesus Christ of Latter-day Saints, October 2007. https://www.churchofjesuschrist.org/study/general-conference/2007/10/good-better-best?lang=eng.

[41] Friedel, Frank, and Hugh Sidey. "Dwight D. Eisenhower." The White House. The United States Government, January 2006. https://www.whitehouse.gov/about-the-white-house/presidents/dwight-d-eisenhower/.

[42] "Eisenhower's Urgent/Important Principle: Using Time Effectively, Not Just Efficiently." Time Management Skills. Accessed April 29, 2020.

https://www.mindtools.com/pages/article/newHTE_91.htm.

[43] Empringham, Tim. "Working Smarter Using the Eisenhower Matrix." Succeed Sooner, November 17, 2017. succeedsooner.ca/2017/04/19/working-smarter-using-the-eisenhower-matrix/.

[44] Palm, Matthew J. "Douglas Carter Beane Looks for the Kindness in New 'Cinderella'." *Orlando Sentinel*, June 16, 2018. www.orlandosentinel.com/entertainment/arts-and-theater/os-cinderella-broadway-douglas-carter-beane-20151103-story.html.

[45] Estevez, Eric. "How did Warren Buffett get started in business?" Investopedia.com, December 22, 2020. https://www.investopedia.com/articles/01/071801.asp

[46] Montini, Laura. "The Offbeat Habits of 7 Famous Leaders." Inc.com., November 21, 2014. https://www.inc.com/laura-montini/7-unorthodox-rituals-of-outstanding-leaders.html

[47] McKay, Brett and Kate. "The Tao of Boyd: How to Master the OODA Loop." Artofmanliness.com, November 6, 2020. https://www.artofmanliness.com/articles/ooda-loop/

[48] Byrum, Joseph. "Allying a Military Model to Financial Chaos." ORMS Today, January 1, 2019. pubsonline.informs.org/do/10.1287/orms.2019.01.01/full/.

[49] *Star Wars: Phantom Menace*. 20th Century Fox, 1999.

[50] McChrystal, Stanley. *Leaders: Myth and Reality*. 1st ed. Vol. 1. New York City, NY: Portfolio/Penguin, 2018.

51 "Highest-Grossing Animation at the Domestic Box Office (Inflation Adjusted)." Guinness World Records. Accessed June 30, 2021. www.guinnessworldrecords.com/world-records/highest-box-office-film-gross-for-an-animation-inflation-adjusted.

52 Pfeiffer, Lee. "Snow White and the Seven Dwarfs." *Encyclopedia Britannica*. Accessed July 2, 2021. www.britannica.com/topic/Snow-White-and-the-Seven-Dwarfs-film-1937.

53 Hayes, Adam. "Six Sigma." Investopedia.com, March 24, 2021. https://www.investopedia.com/terms/s/six-sigma.asp#ixzz5C6xtU1f8

54 Sweeney, Benjamin. "Standard Deviation: What Is Six Sigma?" ClydeBank Media, May 11, 2021. www.clydebankmedia.com/blog/business/process-optimization/what-is-six-sigma.

55 *Companies That Have Successfully Implemented Lean Six Sigma*. MBizM Group, January 11, 2019. www.mbizm.com/companies-that-have-successfully-implemented-lean-six-sigma/.

56 Witnify. "The 1980 Miracle on Ice: Herb Brooks." SBNation.com. SBNation.com, February 11, 2014. https://www.sbnation.com/miracle-on-ice-1980-us-hockey/2014/2/11/5400156/the-1980-miracle-on-ice-herb-brooks.

57 DiMeglio, Denise. "Press Release Restaurants 2019-2020." American Customer Satisfaction Index. June 30, 2020. www.theacsi.org/news-and-resources/press-releases/press-2020/press-release-restaurants-2019-2020.

⁵⁸ Taylor, Kate. "Chick-fil-A Is Taking over America by Offering the Best Customer Service in Fast Food." *Business Insider*, June 26, 2019. www.businessinsider.com/chick-fil-a-best-customer-service-in-fast-food-2019-6.

⁵⁹ "Chernobyl Accident 1986." World Nuclear Association, May 2021. http://www.world-nuclear.org/information-library/safety-and-security/safety-of-plants/chernobyl-accident.aspx.

⁶⁰ "1986-2016: CHERNOBYL at 30." World Health Organization, April 26, 2016. www.who.int/publications/m/item/1986-2016-chernobyl-at-30.

⁶¹ Lawrence, Chris. "31 Victims Identified in Widening Air Force Sex Scandal." CNN.com, June 29, 2012. https://www.cnn.com/2012/06/28/justice/texas-air-force-scandal/index.html.

⁶² Pace, Eileen. "Air Force Announces Results of Investigation into Lackland MTI Sexual Assault Cases." TPR.org. November 15, 2012. https://www.tpr.org/military-veterans-issues/2012-11-15/air-force-announces-results-of-investigation-into-lackland-mti-sexual-assault-cases.

⁶³ Akers, Mick. "BYU Basketball Rumor: Brandon Davies Dismissed for Having Kid on the Way?" BleacherReport.com, March 2, 2011. https://bleacherreport.com/articles/624656-byu-basketball-brandon-davies-dismissed-from-byu-for-having-kid-on-the-way.

⁶⁴ Jaschik, Scott. "The Numbers and the Arguments on Asian Admissions." InsideHigherEd.com, August 7, 2017. https://www.insidehighered.com/admissions/article/2017/08/07/look-data-and-arguments-about-asian-americans-and-admissions-elite.

[65] Hartocollis, Anemona. "Asian-Americans Suing Harvard Say Admissions Files Show Discrimination." *The New York Times*, April 4, 2018. https://www.nytimes.com/2018/04/04/us/harvard-asian-admission.html.

[66] Kirshner, Alex. "An Auburn walk-on's family says NCAA rules make him ineligible because he uses cannabis oil to treat seizures." SBNation.com, May 26, 2018. https://www.sbnation.com/college-football/2018/5/25/17393624/ncaa-marijuana-policy-auburn-cj-harris.

[67] Carroll, Lewis. *The Annotated Alice: Alice's Adventures in Wonderland and Through the Looking-Glass*. Penguin Books, 2012.

[68] Umoh, Ruth. "How the man behind Marvel's 'Avengers' went from washing cars to a $1 billion blockbuster." CNBC.com, May 7, 2018. https://www.cnbc.com/2018/05/04/marvel-president-kevin-feige-went-from-washing-cars-to-the-avengers.html.

[69] *Ready Player One*. Warner Bros. Pictures, 2018.

[70] "Transcript: Barack Obama's DNC Speech." CNN, Cable News Network. August 20, 2020. www.cnn.com/2020/08/19/politics/barack-obama-speech-transcript/index.html.

[71] "Popular Quotes." Air Force Association. Accessed on July 2, 2021. secure.afa.org/quotes/Quotes_81208.pdf.

[72] Jones, Minnie L. "William 'Billy' Mitchell – 'The Father of the United States Air Force.'" U.S. Army, October 17, 2019.

www.army.mil/article/33680/william_billy_mitchell_the_father_of_the_united_states_air_force.

[73] Lucero, Diego. "Why Blockbuster Failed." Siamtek.com. November 7, 2013. https://siamtek.com/why-blockbuster-failed/.

[74] Satell, Greg. "A Look Back at Why Blockbuster Really Failed and Why It Didn't Have To." *Forbes*. Forbes.com, September 5, 2014. https://www.forbes.com/sites/gregsatell/2014/09/05/a-look-back-at-why-blockbuster-really-failed-and-why-it-didnt-have-to/?sh=79114f0c1d64.

[75] McFadden, Christopher. "The Fascinating History of Netflix." Interesting Engineering, July 4, 2020. interestingengineering.com/the-fascinating-history-of-netflix.

[76] "George Washington." History.com. A&E Television Networks, October 29, 2009. https://www.history.com/topics/us-presidents/george-washington.

[77] "Washington's Farewell Address 1796." Avalon Project. Yale Law School. Accessed June 27, 2020. https://avalon.law.yale.edu/18th_century/washing.asp.

[78] Baldoni, John. "The Patriot Way: Do Your Job." *Forbes*. Forbes.com, January 28, 2017. https://www.forbes.com/sites/johnbaldoni/2017/01/28/the-patriot-way-do-your-job/?sh=3b09e81e260d.

[79] Camerota, Christian. "Teaching the Patriot Way to Harvard MBAs." HBS.edu, February 2, 2017. https://www.hbs.edu/news/articles/Pages/patriot-way-wells.aspx.

[80] Allen, Evan. "Belichick Starts Chanting 'No Days Off!' to Many Who Had Taken the Day Off." BostonGlobe.com. The Boston Globe, February 7, 2017. www.bostonglobe.com/metro/2017/02/07/belichick-starts-chanting-days-off-thousands-who-had-taken-day-off/NXDHqAOObzwDwWM37QJFQK/story.html.

[81] "More Brady with Oprah: 'There's Definitely an End Coming...'." NBC Sports, June 16, 2018. www.nbcsports.com/boston/patriots/more-brady-oprah-theres-definitely-end-coming.

[82] Philbrick, Nathanial. "Why Benedict Arnold Turned Traitor Against the American Revolution." *Smithsonian Magazine*. Smithsonianmag.com, May 2016. https://www.smithsonianmag.com/history/benedict-arnold-turned-traitor-american-revolution-180958786/.

[83] "The Battle of Bemis Heights." History.com. A&E Television Networks, March 19, 2010. www.history.com/topics/american-revolution/battle-of-bemis-heights.

[84] "Benedict Arnold: General in the Battle of Saratoga." HistoryNet, January 24, 2018, www.historynet.com/benedict-arnold-general-in-the-battle-of-saratoga.htm.

[85] Arnold, Isaac N. *The Life of Benedict Arnold*. Chicago, IL: Jansen, McClurg, & Company, 1880.

[86] Ferran, Lee. "Why Spy? What Drove Benedict Arnold to Turn Traitor." Insidehook.com, September 21, 2018. https://www.insidehook.com/article/history/spy-drove-benedict-arnold-turn-traitor.

[87] Daniels, Greg, and Michael Schur. "Jerry's Painting." *Parks and Recreation*, 3, no. 11, NBC. April 28, 2011.

[88] "Alexander the Great." History.com. A&E Television Networks, November 9, 2009. https://www.history.com/topics/ancient-history/alexander-the-great.

[89] Wasson, Donald L. "Battle of Gaugamela." World History Encyclopedia, February 27, 2012. https://www.worldhistory.org/Battle_of_Gaugamela/.

[90] Matthews, Rupert. "Battle of Gaugamela." *Encyclopædia Britannica*. Accessed July 2, 2021. www.britannica.com/event/Battle-of-Gaugamela.

[91] *U-571*. Universal Pictures, 2000.

[92] "King George Tells Britons War 'at Doors.'" UPI. Accessed May 19, 2020. https://www.upi.com/Archives/1940/09/23/King-George-tells-Britons-war-at-doors/1481362375108/.

[93] "Mission Belt." Episode. Shark Tank 4, no. 22, June 24, 2013.

[94] "King Louis XVII." Biography.com, April 1, 2014. https://www.biography.com/royalty/louis-xvii.

[95] Featherstone, Vaughn. "The King's Son." Churchofjesuschrist.org. The Church of Jesus Christ of Latter-day Saints. Accessed May 19, 2020. https://www.churchofjesuschrist.org/study/new-era/1975/11/the-kings-son?lang=eng.

[96] Zelizer, Julian E. "The 8 Biggest Unforced Errors in Debate History." POLITICO Magazine, September 24, 2016. https://www.politico.com/magazine/story/2016/09/pres

idential-debates-errors-mistakes-gaffes-biggest-history-214279/.

[97] Markels, Alex. "George H.W. Bush Checks His Watch During Debate with Bill Clinton and Ross Perot." U.S. News & World Report, January 17, 2008. https://www.usnews.com/news/articles/2008/01/17/a-damaging-impatience.

[98] Lee, Harper. *To Kill a Mockingbird*. New York: Warner Books, 1982.

[99] "The Voter's Self Defense System." Vote Smart. Accessed July 2, 2021. justfacts.votesmart.org/candidate/political-courage-test/57111/roy-moore.

[100] "Ten Commandments judge removed from office." CNN, November 14, 2003. http://www.cnn.com/2003/LAW/11/13/moore.tencommandments/.

[101] McCrummen, Stephanie, Beth Reinhard, and Alice Crites. "Woman Says Roy Moore Initiated Sexual Encounter When She was 14, He was 32." *The Washington Post*. WP Company, November 9, 2017. https://www.washingtonpost.com/investigations/woman-says-roy-moore-initiated-sexual-encounter-when-she-was-14-he-was-32/2017/11/09/1f495878-c293-11e7-afe9-4f60b5a6c4a0_story.html?utm_term=.87d54e66d4f9.

[102] Chavez, Nicole, and Jason Hanna. "These Charts Explain How Doug Jones Won in Alabama." CNN, December 13, 2017. https://www.cnn.com/2017/12/13/politics/doug-jones-alabama-win-charts/index.html.

[103] Hackett, Conrad, and David McClendon. "World's Largest Religion by Population Is Still Christianity." Pew Research

Center, April 5, 2017. www.pewresearch.org/fact-tank/2017/04/05/christians-remain-worlds-largest-religious-group-but-they-are-declining-in-europe/.

[104] Rowling, J. K. *Harry Potter and the Deathly Hallows*. London: Bloomsbury, 2014.

[105] "Confidence in Institutions." Gallup.com. Gallup. Accessed May 19, 2020. https://news.gallup.com/poll/1597/confidence-institutions.aspx.

[106] Bennett, Jessica. "Paula Broadwell, David Petraeus and the Afterlife of a Scandal." *The New York Times*, May 28, 2016. https://www.nytimes.com/2016/05/29/fashion/david-petraeus-paula-broadwell-scandal-affair.html.

[107] "Petraeus: What I Learned in Iraq, and How It Applies to Afghanistan." *The Christian Science Monitor*, April 22, 2009. www.csmonitor.com/World/Global-News/2009/0422/petraeus-what-i-learned-in-iraq-and-how-it-applies-to-afghanistan.

[108] "Vivint." Episode. *Undercover Boss* 6, no. 13, February 20, 2015.

[109] Goodwin, Doris Kearns. *Leadership in Turbulent Times*. Thorndike, ME: Large Print Press, a Cengage Company, 2019.

[110] "The Battle of San Juan Hill." History.com. A&E Television Network, March 3, 2010. https://www.history.com/this-day-in-history/the-battle-of-san-juan-hill.

[111] Blue, Matt. "Miami Heat Head Coach Erik Spoelstra's Journey Through the Heat Organization." *Bleacher Report*, May 27, 2011. https://bleacherreport.com/articles/715011-miami-

heat-head-coach-erik-spolestras-journey-through-the-heat-organization.

[112] Gaines, Cork. "How Erik Spoelstra Became the Coach of the Most Powerful Team in Sports Before He Turned 40." *Business Insider*, June 11, 2013. https://www.businessinsider.com/erik-spoelstras-rise-to-heat-head-coach-2013-6#spoelstra-gained-experience-by-serving-as-the-head-coach-for-the-heats-summer-league-team-for-three-seasons-9.

[113] Dwyer, Kelly. "Pat Riley Joined a Late-Night Tape Session with Three Bottles of Wine during Miami's Lowest Finals Moment." Yahoo! Sports. Yahoo!, June 25, 2013. https://sports.yahoo.com/pat-riley-joined-night-tape-session-three-bottles-162622217.html?y20=1.

[114] "Email Surveillance." Episode. *The Office* 2, no. 9, November 22, 2005.

[115] "John McCain in the Military: From Navy Brat to POW." History.com. A&E Television Networks, August 27, 2018. https://www.history.com/news/john-mccain-navy-career-timeline-vietnam-pow.

[116] Carroll, James. "The True Nature of John McCain's Heroism." *The New Yorker*, July 21, 2017. https://www.newyorker.com/news/news-desk/the-true-nature-of-john-mccains-heroism.

[117] Kliegman, Julie. "Reminder: John McCain Refused an Early Release from Prison Camp." *The Week*, July 18, 2015. https://theweek.com/speedreads/567269/reminder-john-mccain-refused-early-release-from-prison-camp.

[118] *The Lion King*. Walt Disney Pictures, 1994.

[119] *Richard Nixon's Top Domestic and Foreign Policy Achievements.* Richard Nixon Foundation. Accessed July 2, 2021. www.nixonfoundation.org/richard-nixons-top-domestic-and-foreign-policy-achievements/.

[120] "1972 United States Presidential Election." Wikipedia. Wikimedia Foundation. Accessed May 20, 2020. https://en.wikipedia.org/wiki/1972_United_States_presidential_election.

[121] Broder, David S. "Nixon Wins Landslide Victory; Democrats Hold Senate, House." *The Washington Post.* WP Company, November 8, 1972. https://www.washingtonpost.com/wp-srv/national/longterm/watergate/articles/110872-1.htm.

[122] "Watergate Scandal." History.com. A&E Television Networks, October 29, 2009. https://www.history.com/topics/1970s/watergate.

[123] "Freida J. Riley." National Museum of Education, December 1, 2005. https://www.nmoe.org/individual/freida-j-riley.

[124] Webster, Ian. "Inflation Rate between 1914-2021." CPI Inflation Calculator, June 10, 2021. https://www.in2013dollars.com/us/inflation/1914.

[125] Nisslon, Jeff. "Why Did Henry Ford Double His Minimum Wage?" *Saturday Evening Post,* January 3, 2014. https://www.saturdayeveningpost.com/2014/01/ford-doubles-minimum-wage/.

[126] "Henry Ford Started the 40-Hour work Week but the Reason Will Surprise You." *IndiaToday.in,* July 27, 2017. https://www.indiatoday.in/education-today/gk-current-affairs/story/40-hour-workweek-henry-ford-1026067-2017-07-27.

127 Klett, Leah MarieAnn. "Southwest Airlines: How faith, servant leadership of Colleen Barrett led to company's massive success." *Christian Post*, January 12, 2019. https://www.christianpost.com/news/southwest-airlines-how-faith-servant-leadership-of-colleen-barrett-led-to-companys-massive-success.html.

128 "What Is Servant Leadership?" Greenleaf Center for Servant Leadership. Accessed July 2, 2021. www.greenleaf.org/what-is-servant-leadership/.

129 Blanchard, Ken. "The Upside-Down Pyramid." Chief Learning Officer, October 11, 2011. https://www.chieflearningofficer.com/2011/10/11/the-upside-down-pyramid/.

130 Knowledge At Wharton. Southwest Airlines' Colleen Barrett on "Servant Leadership." *YouTube*, 2008. https://www.youtube.com/watch?v=6TgR95vnM0c.

131 Hagler, Tyler. "Servant Leadership and the Inverted Pyramid." Servant Leadership and the Inverted Pyramid. May 12, 2018. www.trig.com/tangents/leadership-and-the-inverted-pyramid.

132 *Spartacus*. Universal Pictures, 1960.

133 Bacon, John. "Utah Mayor Brent Taylor killed in latest Afghanistan 'insider attack'." *USA Today*, November 4, 2018. https://www.usatoday.com/story/news/nation/2018/11/04/utah-mayor-brent-taylor-killed-afghanistan-insider-attack/1883961002/.

134 Turkewitz, Julie. "Brent Taylor, Utah Mayor Killed in Afghanistan, Was on 4th Deployment." *New York Times*,

November 4, 2018. https://www.nytimes.com/2018/11/04/us/utah-mayor-killed-afghanistan-brent-taylor.html.

[135] Montero, David. "Utah Town grieves for its mayor, a National Guardsman killed in Afghanistan." *Los Angeles Times*, November 11, 2018. https://www.latimes.com/nation/la-na-mayor-ogden-funeral-20181117-story.html.

[136] Marcotte, David. "2021 Top 50 Global Retailers." NRF, March 24, 2021. nrf.com/blog/2021-top-50-global-retailers.

[137] Cheng, Roger. "Jeff Bezos Is Stepping DOWN: Here Are Some of Amazon's Biggest Accomplishments." CNET, February 7, 2021. www.cnet.com/news/jeff-bezos-is-stepping-down-here-are-some-of-amazons-biggest-accomplishments/.

[138] Kay, Grace. "Amazon Tracks Warehouse Workers' Every Move Because Jeff Bezos Thinks People Are Inherently Lazy, Report Says." *Business Insider*, June 15, 2021. www.businessinsider.com/amazon-polices-based-jeff-bezos-belief-all-workers-are-lazy-2021-6.

[139] Trex, Ethan. "Seven Famous People Who Survived Bankruptcy." CNN. Accessed May 20, 2020. https://www.cnn.com/2008/LIVING/personal/11/19/mf.successful.people.survived.bankruptcy/.

www.ingramcontent.com/pod-product-compliance
Lightning Source LLC
Chambersburg PA
CBHW020643220526
45464CB00001B/272